CAREER DEVELOPMENT
For The College Student

PHILIP W. DUNPHY *(Editor)*
Associate Professor of Cooperative Education
Northeastern University

SIDNEY F. AUSTIN
Director of Career Development and Placement
Northeastern University

THOMAS J. McENEANEY
Graduate and Professional School Counselor
Department of Career Development and Placement
Northeastern University

FIFTH EDITION

 THE CARROLL PRESS
Publishers

43 Squantum St., Cranston, R. I. 02920

About the Authors:

PHILIP W. DUNPHY is an Associate Professor of Cooperative Education and a coordinator of electrical engineering students at Northeastern University and at Lincoln College. For a number of years he was a coordinator of sociology, anthropology and human service students in the College of Liberal Arts at Northeastern University. He received his B.S. from Boston College and his M. Ed. from Northeastern where he has taken advanced courses in counseling theory and practice. Prior to joining the Department of Cooperative Education, he was an assistant to the Dean, Lincoln Institute (now Lincoln College) of Northeastern. He taught high school mathematics and science courses for four years.

SIDNEY F. AUSTIN is Director of Career Development and Placement at Northeastern University. He supervises the career planning and placement program for seniors and alumni of the university. He holds a B.S. in mechanical engineering and an M. Ed. from Northeastern. He joined the Northeastern faculty in 1954 as an instructor of cooperative education, was appointed Assistant Dean and Director of the Department of Cooperative Education in 1968, and Associate Dean of the Division of Cooperative Education in 1970. Before coming to Northeastern he held a variety of positions in aeronautical research with the National Advisory Committee for Aeronautics (now NASA) and the U.S. Air Force at Wright Field, and as an appraiser for Factory Mutual Engineering Division.

THOMAS J. McENEANEY, Graduate and Professional School Counselor in the Department of Career Development and Placement, provides counseling to senior students in the eight colleges who are interested in continuing their education beyond the baccalaureate level. Particular attention is given to those students whose career interests are in the professional fields — dentistry, law and medicine. For over a decade he was responsible for the administration of the on-campus recruiting program of the University. He received his B. S. in business administration and his M. Ed. in counseling and guidance from Northeastern University. He has taken additional courses in human relations, behavioral dynamics and personnel administration at other local universities. For a number of years he was employed in industrial personnel work and was Personnel Manager of Maverick Mills at the time of his appointment to Northeastern. He is a member of the Northeast Advisors to the Health Professions, the National Association of Advisers to the Health Professions, the Northeast Association of Pre-Law Advisers and the Greater Boston and Massachusetts Divisions of the American Personnel and Guidance Association.

© Copyright, 1968, 1969, 1973, 1976 and 1981 by The Carroll Press

Library of Congress Cataloging in Publication Data

Dunphy, Philip W.

    Career development for the college student.

    Bibliography: p
    Includes index.
    1. Vocational guidance — United States. I. Austin, Sidney F., joint author. II. McEneaney, Thomas J., joint author. III. Title.
    HF5382.5.U5D85   1981   378' .19425'0973   80-26933
           ISBN 0-910328-02-1

Manufactured in the United States of America

CONTENTS

CONTENTS — *Continued*

Section III: TECHNIQUES for CAREER IMPLEMENTATION

PREFACE

In undertaking this most recent revision of *Career Development for the College Student*, my fellow authors and I were surprised to find what changes have taken place in the decade and a half since we first conceived the broad outlines for this text. Many basic beliefs have been found shortsighted, the actual balance of world economic power has shifted toward the third world which was not a factor fifteen years ago. Inflation has curtailed the value of salary figures and resulted in our modifying markedly our salary information in Appendix C. Changes in personal life style required recognition throughout the text. Intermediate revisions of the text have attempted to keep abreast of some of these changes over the past fifteen years.

In reviewing the significant changes that have occurred over the lifespan of this text, even authors who see change as normal hesitate in the face of the rapid and seemingly basic effects on our international, national, regional, local and individual goals and values. And yet there is one constant − work. Demands for workers in certain areas have decreased and increased in other areas; specific jobs and job clusters have changed substantially in content, but the work of humans is still the force that produces all that humankind has or is apt to have.

This same period has seen a growing emphasis on career development education at every level. Work-study programs have proliferated. The authors have extensive experience in one educational model which provides such participation. Their experience may be one reason why this text has had a moderate growth of acceptance in a period when the book market has been flooded by a variety of popular books offering simple formulas for success in launching a career. We are grateful to those educators who have brought about acceptance of our approach.

Our students do not seem to concern themselves greatly with the shifting value systems we observe. If there have been changes in their basic values, they are perceivable only in minor social/sexual rearrangements or in more active pursuit of career accomplishments. Truth still has its defenders. Virtue is not without advocates. Light still illumines the open mind. Honesty, persistence, hard work and ingenuity have not vanished from the scene. The quality of our professional-interpersonal involvements has not diminished. Indeed, the majority of our students are concerned with the quality of life more than the quantity of their possessions.

Perhaps because the students' equity in the past is less of a burden than it is for those of us who are older, they can accept the inevitable truth of the human situation: *We cannot go back, we cannot change what was; we must go forward and shape a future which can accommodate a wider range of human world values and goals.*

The technologist, the humanist, the administrator, the leaders and the followers of the decade now upon us and the few years beyond which lead to the end of the century by their adherence to or abandonment of our heritage must shape our national, regional and local destinies. Recent national events indicate some reassessment of priorities which may affect the public service career area but continuing and increasing technological demand will more than balance this emphasis. For the next twenty years, fewer students will be entering and leaving college while the overall demand for trained and learned workers will at least remain stable (if only by the attrition due to retirements) and may even increase. The coming decades will be good years for the college graduate.

With, as always, heartfelt thanks to my fellow authors, my family, my publishers and my readers, I dedicate this edition to the students and counselors who will use it.

PHILIP W. DUNPHY

Boston, Massachusetts
January, 1981

Section I: CAREER THEORY

Chapter One

THE CHANGING WORLD OF WORK

by

Philip W. Dunphy

The Nature of Work

Why do people work?

The question may strike you as frivolous when the answer seems so obvious: "To earn a living."

But men have not always worked to earn a living. The nature of work has changed over the years and so have men's attitudes toward work.

Development of Our Industrial Culture

Primitive cultures are essentially food-centered. Their main drive is obtaining enough food for the population. Once a culture solves its food problems, it almost invariably turns to trade. Only with the advent of industry can a general work concept begin to be developed.

By its nature, industrialism forces labor specialization and trade. An industrial economy must continually improve the efficiency of its food and fabric production to support itself, which explains why the earliest concentration of the industrial revolution was in agriculture and textile production.

As the effectiveness of a machine-centered culture increases, the basic human needs can be left to a smaller percentage of the population, and work diversification with its accompanying specialization is possible. Once the potential specializations are multiplied enough, individuals can have some freedom in choosing occupations independent of the basic needs areas. The body of knowledge and material can be developed with increasing speed and the fruits of the culture become more widely distributed among the people.

In order to accomplish this total industrialization in a minimal time, the material and economic factors must be complemented by a religious or ethical force which supports and reinforces the participation of the population in the goals of industrialism. In our culture, this force is called the "Protestant Ethic". Developing along with the industrial mechanical capability of the West, this ethic can be summarized briefly: Work is good in itself; it is sinful not to work if one is able; and the fruits of work should be distributed according to the contribution of the workers and financiers.

Paradoxically, while we extol the virtues of work, we do everything possible to avoid it. Increasingly sophisticated machines are emancipating men from most manual labor. How will we occupy ourselves in the future when a few workers can operate the entire production capacity of the nation?

Let us examine the forces which brought us to this juncture and what they portend for the future in relation to individual career decisions.

Meaning of Work in an Industrial Culture

More than any other nation, the United States has developed a work-centered culture. This characteristic of our national life is observed by almost any foreign visitor and is considered remarkable by observers from some more remote countries. Not all nations or cultures deify work as we do. In fact, some nations scorn our emphasis on work.

Industrialization and the Protestant Ethic have fueled our economy to such a pitch of productivity that we can no longer separate motive from capability. Thus we all pay homage to the sanctity of work and orient our lives to its force.

Although the word "work" applies to all forms of labor, toil and effort, the phrase "The World of Work" conveys a meaning of employment for which compensation is received.

Some of the terms used in describing the World of Work appear to be inter-changeable—such as Job, Position, Career—but there are actually subtle differences in meaning. A leading guidance author once defined these distinctions as follows.[1]

Position: A group of tasks performed by one person. There are always as many positions as there are workers in a plant or office.

Job: A group of similar positions in a single plant, business establishment, educational institution, or other organization. There may be one or many persons employed in the same job.

Occupation: A group of similar jobs found in several establishments.

Career: A sequence of positions, jobs, or occupations that one person engages in during his working life.

A generation or so ago, most well-educated people could reasonably expect to find their careers in their occupations. The two terms were practically synonymous. This is no longer true for anyone except the least ambitious or the most fortunate.

Several factors have contributed to a condition of uncertainty and transiency in the whole field of career development. The impact of these factors has created two conditions:

(1) Jobs are constantly changing in their nature and requirements. The job a person has today, although it may be called the same as the one he had five years ago, does not involve the same functions, background requirements, roles, or personal skills it did then. Jobs are evolving and being revolutionized with great rapidity.

(2) The old career sequences we have known are no longer valid. Experience has less significant permanent value if the functions and attributes of a job are redefined. A person can no longer prepare for a career, take the entry job of the chain, and just continue to progress on experience alone.

New Trends in the World of Work

In the past, work was assigned either by heredity or selective apprenticeship. Leadership was usually hereditary; other professions and crafts were entered by apprenticeship. The nonspecialist became the farmer, soldier, sailor — or, later, the factory or mine laborer. Assignments were mainly by socioeconomic condition. Ability and wealth were presumed to be interrelated. During the mercantile and early industrial revolution periods, freedom of choice was minimal.

As we have seen in the development of the Industrial Revolution, when men gave up the attempt to be self-sufficient in providing their own basic needs of food and clothing, the era of occupational specialization began.

Specialization

Perhaps the most realistic label for our present era is the "Age of Specialization." There are many reasons for the development of occupational specialization, some of them already indicated, but there are two which deserve attention here:

(1) The rapid advancement in knowledge increment. Some prophets predict that in the not-too-distant future knowledge will double every day. This increase in knowledge is paralleled by an increase in accomplishment, although practice always lags behind theory because action takes longer than thought.

(2) Communication techniques have developed so rapidly that the increasing knowledge can be effectively stockpiled and made accessible to men everywhere.

Let's take an example. Twenty years ago most school systems had teachers, administrators and clerks. The teacher was a specialist in subject matter only, experienced in instructional techniques, and assisted occasionally in the administrative processes. School administration was broad, with one or two persons responsible for finance, personnel, curriculum, discipline and facility planning and implementation.

In a typical school system today, the chief administrator will be concerned with broad policy and public relations. He may have area specialists for fiscal, personnel and curriculum planning. There may exist a whole new structure to deal with student behavior, no longer called "discipline," and a permanent group of specialists to advise on facilities and long-range planning.

Instructional techniques have changed also with the use of multisensory aids, computers, and closed-circuit television. Team teaching is common with new levels of responsibility and new roles for the teacher. Teacher aides now handle much of the non-professional classroom work.

Similar changes are taking place in almost all fields. The specific responsibilities, authorities and roles of the job are being more narrowly defined. Largeness of organization is both expected and desired. New levels of administration and new areas of line and staff function are being created.

Specialization in modern times has been largely specialization of function. Currently, this functional specialization is being complemented by field and method specialization. For example, not many years ago, a doctor was a doctor. Then the functional specialties of surgery, internal medicine, etc., developed. Psychiatry was one of the later functional specialties. Now we find field specialties such as child psychiatry and method specialties such as psychoanalysis.

While we have no effective means of categorizing people except in a general evaluative sense, we can and do label the specializations of work. The current *Dictionary of Occupational Titles*[2] lists approximately 20,000 separate jobs. Each title is, in a sense, a specialty — by function, field and method.

Of the 20,000 or so occupations, about 1,500 concern the first two of ten major categories. These are the "Professional, technical and managerial occupations" within which most college graduates find their careers. This part of the *Dictionary* is the least comprehensive and least fully investigated. It is entirely possible that many titles have been missed.

Specialization has two attendant problems. The first is that *specialization implies depth, and this requires time.* Despite more advances in life expectancy, we have the strange situation in which a person spends an increasing proportion of his or her work life preparing for an occupation.

Second, *specializations quickly become outdated.* Automation is a fact of life not only to the skilled and semiskilled worker but also a fact to be reckoned with by professional, managerial and technical workers who often have to upgrade or even abandon their specialties. For example, computer programmers, who are currently in great demand, may already be slated for obsolescence because a good programmer can program an adequate computer to program both itself and other computers.

A significant number of present specialties will have only historical interest in twenty years. Half the jobs people will hold a decade from now do not exist today.

Automation

One major factor in job and career vulnerability in the last half of the 20th century is automation: the use of machines to perform human tasks of ever-increasing complexity.

Already, many workers in a wide range of professional, managerial and technical pursuits are discovering that their skills are becoming obsolete due to their inability to adapt to and utilize new automated tools. Even some young people graduating in a career field find that their specialty is being phased out.

A forestry graduate, for example, may be assigned to an experiment involving the attempt to generate a universally identical plant population through cloning. Unless his or her background in biology and botany is greater than average, he or she may fail to be aware of the much greater potential biological/environmental sensitivity of this group. Updating is an immediate need.

Such changes mean unemployment and a need to find new career directions for workers with a longer time investment, if they have not kept abreast of the developments in their fields. The emotional and intellectual impact can be traumatic.

Similar crises can be found in almost all technical areas. In managerial fields, many experienced but unadaptable workers have been unable to understand and accept the concepts of computerization, matrix techniques, and constant inventory which are now utilized. Many others have adapted well by acquiring additional education and new skills. Professional people — especially in medicine, education and communications — have faced comparable situations.

Mobility

Social mobility and its accompanying economic mobility is not really novel in American society, but its definite association with job and career is relatively new. Patterns of status, directly related to job or careers, are emerging. Vance Packard in *The Status Seekers* [3] clearly indicates that the most significant single factor in determining status is occupation.

What is happening is that many persons, often not consciously realizing their motivation, are striving toward certain career areas for their status value. In a sense, while the two are often connected, status security is assuming greater importance than economic security for a great many people.

—In our socially and economically mobile society, certain careers have significant status value. The student should be aware of his status goals as well as his economic and social goals.

Associated with this socioeconomic mobility is a trend for workers in low status occupations to seek higher status by forming professional associations with publicized professional requirements; for example, "sanitary engineers" instead of garbage collectors and street sweepers.

Geographical mobility has also led to a marked decrease in the definiteness of commitment of jobs at all levels, including those occupied by the college graduate. Whereas, in the past, a person might locate in a community and commit himself to a lifetime career with a single employer, now he must expect to relocate several times— whether or not he stays with the same employer.

As a concomitant of this company mobility, workers are increasingly initiating moves in seeking further career development opportunity. The norm is no longer one or two job changes in a lifetime. Even in professional, technical and managerial careers, the average number of job changes is between four and five. The flexible person is flexible in geography as well as capability. He goes where the job is, rather than accepting the first job available.

—Geographic mobility—either as a requirement of corporate progress or as means of career opportunity for the individual—must be a conscious aspect of career development.

The Population Explosion

The impact of the population explosion on the World of Work is highly visible in some areas, less so in others. There are more workers to produce goods and, to balance this potential glut, there are more consumers for the goods produced.

But the sociological effects of increasing population are not so neatly resolved. The public first became aware of some of the burdens of population growth when the surge of enrollments put a strain on every public and private school facility. The shock wave has now reached past college to graduate schools and beyond.

Combined with new developments in medical technology which extend the life expectancy of citizens, we have other sociological concerns. The working life for unskilled and semiskilled workers is still cut off far before the period of life is over, despite new legal changes. Geriatrics — both medical and sociological — is now a rapidly growing new field; so is adult and continuing education. Whole communities are being constructed for "senior citizens" and social isolation is a real concern.

At the same time, new services to youth, minority groups and the disadvantaged are increasingly needed. In combination with the goals of educational, economic and social equality, the needs raise many new service opportunities for career seekers.

The Emerging Megalopoli

The "flight from the cities" as a result of transportation changes and population pressures has directed attention to the need for urban redevelopment. The nature and extent of centralized medical services is changing rapidly. Now that we are giving due emphasis to "people problems", the social scientist is able to command both respect and reward. Instead of being an ivory-towered academician, he is now an active participant in the total industrial, governmental and business picture. The specialties within this broad field are proliferating and so are the requirements for each specialty.

The shifting patterns of population are beginning to show what appears to be a definite and probably irreversible trend. We have gone through the period of urbanization and are now well into the era of suburbanization.

What is only beginning to be realized is that suburbia is not an entity in itself, but rather an organic complex of communities. High among the integrating and sometimes disrupting components of suburban complexes are educational and corporate sub-communities. These two cohesive influences are responsible for the new socio-geographic entity—Megalopolis.

There is a whole new dimension of size and scope in socio-economic affairs. Large segments of industry, especially those dealing in the varieties of technology, are actively seeking to locate in large, well-developed metropolitan areas. One prime reason for this deliberate geographical clustering is the accessibility of adequate educational resources. In some cases, the large "brain farms" are the major magnet for industry.

Two important results of this trend are the creation of increasingly larger "megaversities" and increasing concentration of prime government contract moneys. Again, the two go hand-in-hand, each essential to the other. A by-product has been developed: more financial help for students, especially at the graduate level. For both the student and the university, of course, there is the danger of governmental or industrial over-influence. To some extent, education is in danger of becoming a tertiary product of a megaversity, falling behind research and service to both the industrial and social communities.

Regardless of the philosophical question, the fact is that for certain areas of specialization, there is a limited number of really adequate educational resources. The professional persons in these fields and the corporations involved naturally accrue to the educational environment best qualified to serve their needs.

Industrial and Career Trends

A remaining factor for consideration is that some industrial and professional areas are phasing out, others phasing in. Over the past twenty years or more, it has become evident that significant industrial trends and demands have entered the picture.

First, there is a constantly increasing demand for higher levels of education, especially in the technical, professional and managerial areas. This is both a cause and an effect of increased specialization. It can be a source of increased individual flexibility.

The proportion of people with education or training beyond high school is increasing. In addition, specialized post-college education is required more and more.

Second, the number of people at the levels actively engaged in producing goods is falling off; the number involved in providing ideas and services is increasing. This trend is especially noticeable in such service areas as the medical and paramedical fields. Even in fields like space technology, the number of people actively producing goods is not rising as rapidly as those providing auxiliary services such as operations planning.

Theories of Career Choice

In approaching your own career planning and development, it may help you to understand some of the philosophy of career development which has evolved from past experience and present observations.

Divine Intervention

The oldest theory of vocational choice was Divine Selection. A person chosen for a particular career was notified directly by some Superior Being. While not prevalent in our society today, this theory still has many adherents—especially in theological groups where a candidate for leadership has to prove that he or she has been "called" by God.

Heredity

After the Divine Selection theory and as social structures became somewhat formalized, career selection was largely a matter of socio-economic inheritance. While the requirements for certain vocations had to be modified to fit the practitioner's abilities, the Inheritance Theory worked well for earlier economies, although it was hard on many individuals. (Few writings of ancient Greece or Rome mention the careers of the subjugated majority.)

Both of these methods of career selection are still practiced in some parts of the world; for example, in India. In a rapidly changing society, however, such deterministic methods are ineffective in meeting the needs of the economy or the individual.

Several theories of vocational determination are still accepted in whole or in part and so deserve attention.

Chance

A belief in Chance as a career determinant is the secular equivalent of the theory of Divine Selection. Fundamentally, it goes as follows: A person is born, grows, learns, observes his environment, and at some point seizes a passing career opportunity. The careers of many competent and economically successful people give evidence of the sometime success of this theory.

Carried to a logical extreme, however, this idea is inconsistent with the self-development of the individual. Nevertheless, *there is no question that unforeseen circumstances almost always play some part in career choice and development for almost everyone.*

Socio-Economic Determinism

This is the old theory of Inheritance brought up-to-date. It says that what a person becomes is substantially determined by what his parents did for a living, the economic level of the family and its status, and the security of the individual.

A career may be influenced by Socio-Economic Determinism directly by following in the family tradition or, indirectly, by rebelling against the tradition and seeking a higher or—sometimes—lower socio-economic status.

While inadequate as a complete pattern for career choice and development in our contemporary society, *socio-economic circumstance does have a significant effect on an individual's choice and pursuit of a career.*

Psychological Determinism

This relatively modern (19th century) theory comes in several shades, the most extreme being that career choice is unconsciously or subconsciously determined by the early training and environment of the child.

Carried to an extreme interpretation, the application of this theory would permit the claim of some analytical psychologists that surgeons and butchers are sublimating sadistic tendencies, policemen and army officers are sublimating hidden aggressions, etc. Such a hypothesis is certainly open to question. However, as in most other theories of career selection, there is a kernel of truth. *People are affected by emotional experiences in their choice of careers; and there are psychological limitations which restrict our selection of occupational pursuits.*

Trait and Factor Matching

This more recent and still common theory is also centered in psychology, but in the objective, statistical, testing areas of the science rather than the subjective, analytical field.

In effect, the theory is as follows: A job can best be chosen by first analyzing one's self—listing abilities and limitations, strong and weak points, likes and dislikes—and then analyzing various jobs in terms of duties, responsibilities, personal requirements, etc. The theory has recently been expanded to cover social and economic factors of the individual and job. (See the next theory.)

There is no question that Trait and Factor Matching is a far better way to select a career than chance; but the student should realize that this theory has certain limitations which cannot be overcome.

First, it is a theory of job choice, not of career development. It assumes that job and career are substantially the same, which is no longer true.

Second, it assumes that devices (tests, inventories, interviews, etc.) are able to provide adequate self-information, which is very doubtful.

Third, the theory implies limitations without specifying them. Applied at the end of high school, for example, few economically deprived students would even be aware of many jobs which might well suit their latent abilities and interests.

Within these limitations, however, the student may find the information about self and jobs discovered in the Trait and Factor Matching approach of some value in career planning.

Developmental Theories

Most recent in the theoretical hierarchy are several theories which jointly state the following: As a person develops from birth, he follows a general pattern of development. His needs change; his desires change; his abilities and disabilities are defined; he assumes new roles and abandons old ones; and through all of this development he "becomes" a person. His choice of career is made, then, with his knowledge of his personal needs, abilities, and experience plus a general knowledge of the capacity of some careers to satisfy these needs, to utilize and to give value to his experience, without regard to current career opportunities.

In other words, the individual's choice of a career is part of his total development as a person.

Obviously, this approach to career development offers a more comprehensive frame work than any of the previously described theories. Its chief drawback is that it places too much emphasis on the individual's internal conditioning toward a career without taking into account sufficiently the limitations of external environment. Thus, we come to a multi-dimensional theory which incorporates features from previous theories and adds some new dimensions.

A Multi-Dimensional Approach to Career Development

Remembering that "flexibility" is the key word to career development in the Changing World of Work, we believe there are four dimensions to be kept in mind:

(1)   *Self*—You must understand your own personal interests, abilities, needs and values.

(2)   *Environment*—You must acquaint yourself with the available career opportunities and requirements.

(3)   *Time*—You must be prepared to make decisions which bring the first two dimensions into focus at a specific time.

(4)   *Process*—You must condition yourself to a lifelong series of specific decisions based on the periodic convergence of the first three dimensions. You can visualize this fourth dimension easily if you compare "Process" to a high-speed camera which takes sequence shots of a marathon runner. Each flash picture shows the same runner but in a different position, a different geographical place at a different time. Yet all of the pictures are of the same race.

Summary and Conclusions

What meanings do all of these changes and trends have for the college student? Potentially they are of great importance. In general, a career today is a less easily isolated concept than it was in the past.

Change is natural; stability is no longer a value in itself.

The person now preparing for a career must have increasing definition of goals, tentativeness of commitment, and the ability to relate to a multidisciplinary structure.

Education is no longer a preliminary preparatory stage of career development; it is a continuing, almost constant pursuit of the skilled person. Flexibility can be maintained only by constant updating of background and skills and by periodic review of the individual's goals, directions, and even values. Automation has made techniques more subject to change.

A person must expect to change location, job, function or role with increasing frequency.

FOOTNOTES

1.   Carroll L. Shartle, *Occupational Information: Its Development and Application,* third edition, (c) 1959, pages 22-24. Reprinted by permission of Prentice-Hall, Inc., Englewood Cliffs, New Jersey.

2.   *Dictionary of Occupational Titles,* 4th edition. United States Government Printing Office, Washington, D.C. 1977.

3.   Vance Packard, *The Status Seekers.* N.Y., David McKay Co., Inc., 1959.

Chapter Two

ANATOMY OF A CAREER DECISION

by

Philip W. Dunphy

Part I

CAREERS and PEOPLE

Career development is a process of successive approximation. Goals change, and actions suited to achieving goals change. There are points at which it is essential to select one course of action and reject others.

The essential element in the career process is decision. A decision is a choice of one from two or more alternatives. Each choice is made at a particular point in time based on the available knowledge of career opportunities and requirements, and an awareness of personal interests, abilities, needs and values.

Basic Orientation

Each occupation establishes a relationship between the worker and his external environment. The environment is composed of People, Things and Ideas.

Occupations can be described in terms of the relative weight of each of these factors—People, Things and Ideas. "Numbers" can be treated either as "Things" in a concrete sense or as "Ideas" in an abstract sense. Each occupation at a professional, technical, or managerial level involves at least some minimum amount of each factor.

Within a group of related occupations, the relative emphasis on the People-Things-Ideas factor can differ. For example: A medical doctor is necessarily involved with People, Things (drugs, instruments, etc.) and Ideas (data, diagnostic constructs, etc.). The general practitioner may place the most significant weight on the inter-personal relationship (People factor). The surgeon tends to place a higher emphasis on the Thing factor (organs, muscles, physiological structure, etc.). And the specialist in internal medicine, or psychiatry, deals primarily with Ideas in the form of data, concepts, and empathetic understanding.

The weight that each person assigns to People, Things, or Ideas is largely determined by his early experience which reflects itself in his interests and values and in his choice of pre-college, college undergraduate and graduate fields of study.

Determining the Basic Orientation

For most college-age young people, the choice of courses and extra-curricular activities has already pointed the way toward some career field. Although there is no perfect balance of interests and abilities for a particular career, interest should be accompanied by some degree of skill or potential. For example, the student who would love to design a bridge but cannot master trigonometry should re-examine his career orientation to discover a better utilization of his interests.

A Note on Creativity

To this point we have not mentioned the creative person. The reasons are simple—he is hard to define and identify. In a general sense, however, creativity is the ability to do something new, and applies to either "People", "Things", or "Ideas". The creative counselor will find new ways to help his client achieve insight and clarity. The creative architect will find new uses and materials and forms to express his thoughts. The creative researcher will phrase new theories to explain the already explained and resolve a bit of the incomprehensible.

Activities

Having now discussed the concept of basic orientation, we can with a great deal of honest self-searching, ascribe to ourselves some relative balance of orientation toward People, Things or Ideas. But this is much too broad a categorization to be really helpful in seeking occupations.

Within each of the basic orientations and combinations thereof can be found certain types of functions or activities. As with our previous section, the difficulty we face is that in stating some of these, we will omit others. In general, the functions listed for each orientation form a hierarchy—the topmost requiring the greatest ability and skill.

Within each of the following categories, the list is broken to indicate the appropriate division of high involvement from moderate involvement:

People Oriented Activities
Maintaining-Adjusting (Therapy)
Coordinating (Counseling)
Instructing
Supervising
  Persuading
  Communicating (Serving input)

Thing Oriented Activities
Designing
Developing
Fabricating (Prototype-Pilot Plant)
Refining (Improving)
  Setting up; Precision fabricating
  Operating Controlling

Idea Oriented Activities
Generating (Creating)
Synthesizing
Coordinating
Analyzing
  Compiling (Accumulating)
  Computing (Summarizing)

Levels of Preparation and Degrees of Involvement:

The degree of involvement which exsists between a person and his occupation is directly, though not solely, related to the amount of preparation required, the totality of the occupation's demand on the person, and the degree of personal responsibility required.

Within a given career area or field it is usually possible to identify different levels of responsibility, preparation, demands, and—therefore—involvement.

In the area of occupations for college graduates, only two or at most three of six common levels of involvement are pertinent:

Level	Definition
1	Professional, Technical and Managerial, Higher
2	Professional, Technical and Managerial, Regular
3	Semiprofessional, Managerial, Lower

The semiskilled and unskilled categories do not apply (at least in theory). The breaks in our previous list of People—Things—Ideas activities will generally divide the upper two from the lower two categories of level; i.e., Professional from semiprofessional and skilled.

Part II

FACTORS OF SUCCESS

Among others, the following personal factors are directly related to career success in almost all cases:

1. Interests
2. Abilities
3. Goals and Values
4. Knowledge, Training and Experience
5. Energy level.

Interests

Most of the first part of this chapter comprises a discussion of interests. Essentially a person must determine the direction of his interests (People, Ideas, Things); the type of activity he finds most attractive, and the degree of involvement in his career which will bring him adequate satisfaction.

This is the basic step and all others follow from it. Unfortunately, this is also the most difficult step, since only persons who seek some familiarity with various career areas through experience or extensive investigation are really prepared to assess their own interests with any degree of real knowledge. Because of this, problems often arise. Professional counseling is strongly advised in problem cases. Uncertainty of interests or unduly romanticized views of career fields may lead to much wasted time and much unhappiness in career development. It is extremely important to avoid persistent error at this point.

Abilities

As in the case of interests, abilities may not be clearly defined for many persons. To an extent, abilities have been tested in some ways during the school and college years. However, in outline and summary, the following points deserve attention.

Intelligence

Intellectual or mental ability is only one kind of ability. To be sure, certain occupations or careers require minimum degrees of some specific intellectual capacity. Intelligence, however, is currently being reassessed not merely as "mental" or verbal-numerical ability, but as a more general "personal" ability.

Many people do not use their full abilities. As a result, they are not actually aware of what they can do. In some cases, "abilities" can be tested and defined statistically. But the fact that one has ability does not lead to success. Success is attained through the use not the possession of ability.

Personal Relations

In addition to either general or specific intelligence, there are other abilities equally or often more important in finding and following a career. One of these is the ability of a person to interrelate with others. This is somewhat an index of the temperature of personality—warm, accepting, vs. cold, rejecting. As in mental ability, personal or interpersonal abilities are not always used to their fullest. Many of us feel better able to deal with people than we do.

Unfortunately, tests of interpersonal ability are only in their infancy, and we must depend more heavily on experience than on statistics in assessing this factor. As in the case of mental abilities, it is the way we use our abilities to interact with others, not merely knowledge of how we should act, that is most important in shaping our future as it has shaped our past.

Emotion

Closely related to both our mental and our interpersonal abilities are our emotional abilities. Emotion can be loosely conceived as the antithesis of intellect. Intellect deals with ideas, numbers, symbols. Emotion is physical. It deals with feelings, reactions, and its own learned reality. In a sense, each of us has an "Emotional Quotient," a sort of limit on his ability to manage his emotions. This is determined by both his heredity (physical) and his experience.

While the author disagrees with authorities who indicate that abilities are "frozen" early in life, it is not unusual for a person to have his emotional pattern fairly well fixed by the time he enters late adolescence. Emotion often determines the way a person thinks or the way he deals socially with others, in short, his reaction to situations. As a result, emotion is the most significant factor in setting the degree of stress acceptable to an individual in his career. Emotion, whether happy or unhappy, provides energy. But unhappiness leads to additional negative results which may make a person very effective but are much more likely to render him less effective.

To cite two fairly well agreed upon examples: Many serious functional digestive disorders result from emotional conflict. More people worry themselves to an early demise than die from overwork.

The following outline may help to stimulate your own thinking and analysis of your current abilities:

A.   Intelligence:
    1.   General I.Q. relates to overall academic performance; general intelligence tests.
    2.   Numerical-data relates to ability to comprehend, analyze, summarize, interpret numerical data, statistics, etc.
    3.   Verbal correlates with reading ability; ability to communicate well in words, spoken or written.
    4.   Functional—ability to work with tools, hands, hand-eye coordination; observing and interpreting real physical situations.

B.   Interpersonal:
    1.   Ability to relate with individuals: sympathy, empathy; acceptance-rejection; warmth-coolness; closeness-remoteness; directive-non-directive.

    2.   Ability to work as part of a group: cooperation-friction; closure (completing work started); leadership; followship; biases; patience; satisfaction - frustration; coordination-persuasion-manipulation.

    3.   Ability to follow others: see above, especially cooperation; satisfaction; closure.

    4.   Ability to supervise others: see above, especially coordination-persuasion-manipulation; also acceptance, warmth, etc.

C.   Emotional:
    1.   Degree of stability: hyperemotional-apathetic; specific uncertainties; phobias (fears); specific areas of confidence.
    2.   Types of emotional reaction: submissive-aggressive; assertive-timid; degree of emotional judgement and control; sexual adjustment; fixations.

Besides the factors mentioned, certain occupations may require physical, moral, or intellectual courage. Emotional and social risk must also be considered. Each person must see himself as truly as possible in all ways. Only then can he know what he can do, may do, and will do. **The ultimate ability is the ability to use other abilities effectively**.

Goals and Values

The third of the internal factors involved in our choice of career is related to what we hope to achieve through a career. The goals we seek and the values we consciously or unconsciously strive for are among the most difficult of the human factors to define. Part of this difficulty stems from the fact that the American economy is so distinctly materialistic. As a result, material goals and values receive common verbal acceptance. The existence of psychosomatic problems among highly paid executives, however, indicates that material values are not always the only or even the most important of the values men and women really seek through work. Therefore, we will discuss, in addition to material goals, goals and values of service to others and of self-satisfaction.

Material Values:

Many Americans have no real concept of how markedly better their standard of living is than that found in many other parts of the world. Recent awareness of this disparity—brought about by new media of communication—is forcing a value crisis in our nation. There is a great deal of evidence that supports the contention that the basic values of our economy are not nearly as materialistic as they seem. Although this is essentially a profit-oriented economy, the largest part of the "profit" may not be economic. Regardless of current contention, money values are set on work. Closely, almost universally, entwined with the money values are status values. Except for rare fields such as organized crime and religion, high pay and high status go hand in hand.

As a general rule, the money value of occupations follows the rule of supply and demand or of high pay for long periods of preparation. The student is well advised to look clearly at his own thinking and experience regarding the relative weight he places on money-status income.

It is pertinent here to note that where previously the upper salary and status levels in industry and business were reserved largely for the administrator, there is developing a parallel pathway through specialization. An increasing premium is being placed on ability and experience of a nonadministrative type.

Increasing "professionalism" is bringing several previously low ranking fields (teaching, law enforcement, nursing, social work, etc.) up significantly in both pay and status. In these and other "professional" fields, advancement is often accompanied by worker organization and action. Clearly, in some instances, professional and material goals are not always compatible.

Service Values (Humanitarian):

In line with our last paragraph, it is astounding to realize (as our critics seem not to) that our materialistic culture persists in spawning a large percentage of people who compulsively ignore both salary and status and seek jobs and careers which can be defended only by a humanitarian motive. The whole mechanism of federal government is composed of such selfless cogs. So are our schools, social agencies, town, city and state administrations, hospitals, churches and other nonprofit but useful corporate adjuncts.

If there is a student reader who has not met persons of remarkable ability and energy in those fields, he is either very unaware or very unfortunate. For these people who, we often say carelessly "couldn't run the rat race", are the ones who strive at all times to provide the services our economy supports and most other economies do not support as well if at all.

For persons of this caliber, there is some greater value than the economic. This value, whatever it may be, is seen differently by different evaluators. Yet the essence remains that most of these people enter the field they do because they hold some widely differing view of what is important.

Too often counselors have seen students, approaching an occupational choice, strive to ignore their feelings and force themselves to look at the economics of the choice. Certainly the economics of choice are extremely important—but, just possibly, there is a human aspect of economy which should not be thoughtlessly ignored. It is a comforting thought that perhaps a better definition of these human values will come from the present questioning of our value structure. Hopefully, this can be achieved without destroying the material structure which uniquely makes consideration of other values possible.

Self-Satisfaction:

In every class the author has taught, there has been at least one student who consistently does some odd, useless thing because "it could be done." These same individuals seem also to persist in thinking new thoughts. Theirs is a restless heritage, yet one which may, we hope, bring them satisfaction. It is through such people that the great strides in knowledge, technology, application, and even administration are made. They theorize new theories, they find new medicines, they sometimes (rarely) even get elected to high office. They climb mountains "because they are there." They march to the different drummer. They seek their own value—the value of knowing they have done something no one before them did. Such persons should be sure they are not merely wandering in a silence of values.

Knowledge, Training and Experience

In contrast with the previous factors discussed, the requirements of preparation for a career are relatively easy to measure. These are extrinsic to the person. Since there is such a wide variation of specific requirements among careers and jobs, we will mention only basic factors. Of these, the most pertinent are education, skills, and experience.

Education

Until recently, education was a preliminary requirement for an occupation. It usually terminated when the job started. This is no longer the case. One of the pervading realities of almost all occupations today is that education is a part of work. In one form or another, formally or informally, education goes on and on. Even corporate presidents create their own "in-service" training programs.

Formal education is presented in several ways:

1. Formal study for advanced degrees (Master, Doctor).
    a. Specialized—e.g., M.Ed., D.Ed. for teachers.
    b. Diversified—e.g., M.B.A. or L.L.B. for an educational administrator.

2. Up-dating, or "State of the Art" courses (either for credit or not). Common especially in technical fields or in acquainting users with new peripheral technologies and techniques; e.g., even for medical doctors.

3. Training programs combined with some formal education courses but slanted specifically toward a particular, useful combination of knowledge and skill.

Informal education is presented in such situations as:

1. Conventions—becoming less "happy time" more real "work". Sharing of ideas with peers, even competitors.

2. Seminars—replacing the "think-fest". A more structured sharing session. Often involves skill training also.

3. Professional membership—journals, society meetings, active participation encouraged.

4. Lectures by authorities.

5. Workshops.

While some aspects of continuing education are pertinent only after an occupation has been found, some previous concern such as undergraduate professional society participation is looked for by employers.

Skills

Inaccurately, but frequently, "education" means learning of theory. Skills are the applications of theories and are often expected to be learned by experience. In these complex times, however, this is not left to chance or whimsy. Rather, skill training is provided. Among the skill areas involved in some occupations are the following:

1. Interpersonal skills. Developed by seminar participation, committee and workshop membership; professional organizations activity; "sensitivity" training, etc.

2. Application skills. The required skill to perform, not merely propose the operation. Often involves internship (medicine, education, law, nursing, law enforcement), or supervised work (computer programming, college fellowships) etc.

3. Specific behavior skills—e.g., salesmanship, leadership, writing, speaking, listening, even thinking. Encouraged by courses, lectures, assignments, etc.

Experience

A common anecdote in education relates to the comparison of two teachers in a school system. Each had spent thirteen years in teaching. In drawing up references for the two, the superintendent compared them in this way:

> "Jane has had thirteen years of experience as a teacher; John has had one year of experience as a teacher — thirteen times."

Experience is thus no automatic happening, but something which must be consciously considered, formulated, directed. In all occupations, there is a point of diminishing return for experience. For example, in industry a traffic manager may be needed. A company may be willing to hire a person with a year's experience. The same employer may be anxious to get a person with two or three years of experience. A premium will be offered — maybe a big one. But, after three years, no further premium will be offered, even to a man of ten years' experience.

One of the important considerations, then, is "How much experience is enough?" In the last chapter we will discuss this further. As a general rule, when you do a job for a second time the way you did it once before, experience has ended and rote memory is in control.

Energy Level

Occupations and careers differ significantly in the demand they place on the total resources of the individual. Success is dependent upon achievement, which in turn is related to the amount of energy a person expends. Because of the critical importance of this factor, we have allotted a separate discussion to it, even though it corresponds to personal physical ability.

Energy is expended in many different ways. Not all of these ways are physical. Energy output is also connected with emotional satisfaction or dissatisfaction, mental stress, social rapport, nervous balance and other factors.

Each person should, therefore, look at his areas of career interest and at himself in terms of energy requirements and availability. In general, the energy expenditure required by an occupation is directly proportional to three factors: the time of preparation and degree of selectivity (e.g., medical doctors); the responsibility and degree of supervision exercised (e.g., executives); or the type of clientele and scope of problems encountered (e.g., clergy, social service workers).

Some people thrive in the climate of constant demand and availability. They languish if the telephone doesn't ring at 3:00 A.M. Crisis is their diet. Others find their primary joy in a well ordered day, a definite starting time and ending time, a planned personal economy. As is true of other variables, most of us fall between these extremes.

Within any given career area, it is entirely possible to find a situation consistent with the energy level a person has. It is an error to commit yourself to too much or too little energy demand in your work. In looking at your abilities, therefore, keep in mind such questions as:

1. How well am I? Where and what are my physical, emotional, nervous strong and weak points?

2. What specific types of activity do I like? dislike? do well? do poorly?

3. What is my sleeping and waking pattern? How much sleep, rest, relaxation, diversion, do I require? desire?

4. What proportion of my energy and resources do I want to expend in work? In hobbies and other interests? In family activities?

Similarly, each level and type of activity within a career field demands different types and amounts of energy expenditures. In viewing an occupation, this should be considered. For example:

1. What are the hours, environmental conditions, degrees of consistency required?

2. How much free time will I have? How free?

3. What are the emotional demands of the job?

Take, for instance, a student who chooses the medical field but finds, as many do, that he responds poorly to the situation of being constantly on call, out at all hours and in all weather and persistently under tension. There are areas of medicine in which those conditions are much moderated; e.g., dermatology, plastic surgery, pathology, drug research, etc.

There are fields in which it seems virtually impossible to control the energy demands, however. The person who seeks to master his work and not let his work master him should ordinarily avoid entrepreneurship or high level executive jobs. If you are where the "buck" stops, you must always be available to the buck passer.

Part III

THE PROCESS OF DECISION

General

There are a number of ways in which decisions may be achieved. Three of these will be discussed. Since the fundamental criterion of a decision system is its success, this is not meant to imply that any other decision system which works for a person should not be used.

The nature of the decision process is fundamentally the same, regardless of the conscious or unconscious mechanics of decision. A decision is a choice of one from a group of two or more real, available alternatives. The way in which a choice is determined will depend upon the viewpoint and belief of the decision maker. Three approaches are common.

External Determinism

This approach is based on the belief that there is one "right" choice. A person adopting this system is actually acting as though a pre-determined, externally ordained "fate" had dictated a diagram of his life and, thus, his purpose as an individual was to discover and adhere as closely as possible to this pattern. In effect he has accepted an external value system and external determination.

Such a philosophy may lead to two divergent behaviors: Fatalism ("It doesn't matter what I choose—I might as well toss a coin."); or Logical Positivism ("There is only one right choice and I must choose it.")

In the case of the fatalist, decision is equivalent to chance or inevitability and he accepts no responsibility and takes no initiative in the decision process, permitting decisions to be made for him often by default. Such a person does not weigh the alternatives. He accepts the comfortable and easy solution.

In the other extreme, the person following a Logical Positivism philosophy is likely to be over concerned about any apparent errors in decision. His approach is the opposite of the comfortable and easy solution accepted by the fatalist and yet both are relying on external determination.

Internal Determinism

A person using this approach to decision-making refuses to accept any factors as significant except the internal, primarily affective, experience he has in his consciousness. To a certain extent, this is also a one-way outlook, but it is based on non-determinism. The basic assumption is that there is no continuum between decisions; i.e., what is good today may be better or worse tomorrow—it all depends on "me" the individual.

A person making a decision in this manner will usually analyze the present experience field and project his responsibility; then he will choose according to his present experience weight—accepting the right and responsibility to choose and also the right to decide not to choose. Conversely, he will expect to be responsible for his choice and its impact on himself and others.

Effectively what is temporary here is the individual's value system. He refuses to accept any values as more than temporary, experiential factors. The value elements in his model stem from the decision situation as he personally perceives it.

Situational Determinism

The third approach is one in which the problem of choice is related to the individual's internal makeup and his external environment in a systematic and logical way. It has some factors of permanence, a value definition which is more or less consistent and objective. It also has relationship to the "situational" structure since each choice must be analyzed in the here and now even though the results must be predicted over a period of time. The consideration is not only for now and the future, but also for the past; i.e., the background of present and persistent external responsibilities is admitted.

Satisfying choices, within the boundaries of choice available, can be made on the basis of values. Some degree of structure can be built into the process of decision. Note that we consider decision as a process, not an end. We will devote the remainder of the chapter to this process as it applies to career development.

Career Decision

While decisions occur in all of our lives daily, there are certain types of decisions which relate significantly to career development. Among these are:

1. Choice of the first job;
2. When or whether to change jobs;
3. When or whether to change employers;
4. Educational decisions while employed;
5. When or whether to change career direction.

While the types of decisions differ in details, the basic process of decision can be outlined in general terms for a wide variety of applications. The steps can be stated as follows:

1. **Statement of the problem or question.** The word "problem" is used to indicate a point of decision—a statement that some one course of action must be followed to the exclusion of others.

This step leads directly to—

2. **Statement of alternatives.** This requires research into real, available courses of action which may be feasibly followed. This aspect may be very time-consuming and difficult.

The next two steps are interrelated and feed back into each other.

3. **Projection of outcomes.** What is likely to be the immediate, intermediate or long-range effect on my career if I follow each alternative? and—

4.   **Value assignment**. What weight can I assign to each alternative in terms of satisfaction of my immediate, intermediate and long-range goals and values? then—

5.   **Comparison of projections and values**. This is actually the point of selection of the most valuable alternative. This must then be compared affectively (how does it "feel"?).

In practice, each of the steps has some subtle points to be considered.

Statement of the Problem

This seems straightforward, but are you stating the real problem or only a symptom? For example, at the point of graduation many students consider graduate school for the first time. The "problem" then becomes: What field of graduate study? What school? Experience indicates that fair proportion of such graduates are actually masking more basic questions such as, "I don't want to leave the protection of college" or "How will I get a job?" The basic problem in these cases is not "What graduate school?" but "What will I do? How?"

The statement of the problem requires honesty and considerable self-awareness. Masking of real problems does not stop at graduation. There are people who state their problems twenty years later in such phrases as, "I need more money" or "I want more challenge." What they may really be expressing is, "How can I gain more status or responsibility?" or "How can I avoid growing old?"

Except in persistent cases of self-deception, problems generally involve one or more of the following basic needs:

(a)   Need to know facts—jobs, careers, professional or academic requirements, sources of information, etc.

(b)   Need to know how to take a course of action—to write a resume, seek interviews, conduct one's self in situations, write application letters, etc.

(c)   Need to know self—values, goals, abilities, interests, directions.

Because of the large potential for error at this point and the significant psychological blocking which can occur, it is wise in all cases of serious difficulty to seek qualified professional counseling. Self-deception or confusion at this point can create grave errors of action.

Statement of Alternatives

Remembering that the alternatives must define real, available courses of action makes this chore a little less burdensome. This is essentially an information-seeking step. If the student can act with relative freedom and objectivity at this point, the decision process is well on its way to completion.

Defining alternatives is the most creative step in the process. The student who thoroughly and objectively analyzes himself in terms of orientations, abilities, goals and values, and energy level can often rapidly narrow down his field of specific choice. He can then seek information about the opportunities consistent with his personal success factors. There are, however, two important error potentials here.

(a) **Mismatching.** No other factor is a more pervasive cause of career discontent than aiming too high or too low. The student or graduate must be extremely thorough and careful in determining the proportion of his life that his career will involve. If he seeks too little, he will not likely achieve much more than he seeks. Boredom, self-depreciation and lethargy may result. If he seeks too much, either health or pride is almost sure to suffer.

(b) **Inadequate information.** No error is more frustrating than to act on information, achieve a goal, and then find it is not what you thought. All sources of information should be thoroughly investigated. All feasible alternatives should be stated.

Projection

This is, at best, an indefinite process, but it should be done as well as possible. Information used in projection should be current. Projection is actually a statement of future alternatives available, success of job performance, and of significant occupational trends. The factors of success must be applied in succession to all the alternatives, realistically. Vagueness should be minimized. At this point, particularly, the *opinions* of persons in the occupation under consideration may be very helpful. But do not accept their *judgement* unconditionally. According to legend, Albert Einstein was considered a poor student by some of his teachers.

One factor not previously mentioned in detail is pertinent here—the dilemma of freedom vs. commitment. If, as is often the case, a course of action will put additional restrictions on later changes of direction, it should be accompanied by increased value.

In projecting probable outcomes, the questions of likelihood of success and accomplishment should encompass the immediate future (first year or two), the intermediate future (three to five years), and the long-range future (five years to retirement). You might ask such questions as: "If I achieve maximum success, what opportunities will come open next?" or "If I achieve only average success, how far can I expect to go?" "Will I be able to get out of this occupation if I find I don't like it? What can I do then?" While enthusiasm is both important and pleasant, it is best to err on the side of conservatism in making projections.

Value Assignments

No aspect of choice is more important or more difficult than placing a specific value on each alternative. It is difficult enough, though feasible, to project and assign a dollar value (being conservative). And, if this were all that was necessary, no overwhelming problems would arise. But it is only the beginning. Even the subsequent step of assigning a status value is very complex. When such values as "peace of mind", "accomplishment", "achievement", "honor", and even "usefulness" are considered, the problem becomes almost overwhelming. It is at this point in the process of decision that almost everyone at sometime admits, "I don't really know how much I'd like . . . " Yet, it is also at this point that good solid occupational information and adequate awareness of personal values can be joined to set real differential values on alternatives. Without even going to the formal comparison, some alternatives will be rejected here.

Although caution may be redundant, students are again urged to consider all factors of value, not only the material. Unless a person seeks income and benefits far beyond the norm, the actual differences in income from most occupations may not be very great, except for self-employed professionals. In any given occupation there are some "top" jobs which place a person among the elite. If the occupational choice satisfies other values, your chances of achieving maximum material benefits are improved.

Comparison and Selection

If all of the decision-making steps up to this point have been taken carefully, the choice is almost automatic. Problems sometimes arise, however: to cite an instance—which is more important, $50 more a month in salary or 30 minutes less commuting time each way?

When, as may happen, two or more alternative choices compare very closely in value, it is time to go back to the projection and value assessment and dig a little deeper. If the alternatives are occupational, aspects of growth rate, security, rate of progression, etc., may differ between the two opportunities. The same factors can be considered when comparing jobs or employers but here the important factors may be hard to investigate. Given otherwise equal weight, the situational aspects of two jobs may assume greater importance. Can you arrange to visit the employer again to talk further with your supervisor-to-be and get the "feel" of the atmosphere? What is the relative pace of the two opportunities? In some ways, this is an ideal choice—selecting between two good opportunities.

Sometimes the choice is far from ideal—selecting between two poor opportunities. If time and conditions permit, the same course of further action is indicated. Do not resign yourself to failure because alternatives are restricted right now. No choice is really final. There is always another waiting or about to be created. Opportunity may be subject to the vagaries of chance. It is not a piece of gold waiting to be found by the fortunate. It is a decision waiting to be approached by the active seeker.

Section III: AREAS of OPPORTUNITY

Chapter Three

AREAS OF OPPORTUNITY
A Brief Survey of College-level Occupations
by
Philip W. Dunphy

The *Dictionary of Occupational Titles,*[1] frequently referred to in this book, lists over 20,000 different occupations in its current edition. In this chapter we will attempt to survey only a selection of broad career fields in which there are occupations generally requiring a college education or the equivalent.

In Chapter Two we pointed out that all jobs involve activities that are "people" oriented, "thing" oriented or "idea" oriented — often a combination of all three with emphasis on one. Jobs in the professional, technical and managerial categories require that the job holder function in one or more of these aspects (data or ideas, people and things) at a moderate or high level.

Included in the information about specific career fields analyzed in the charts which follow, you will find a notation of the highest function involved under the three headings: Data, People and Things. The *Dictionary of Occupational Titles* identifies a hierarchy of these functions as follows:

Hierarchy of Job Relationships with Data, People, Things

Data (Ideas)	*People*	*Things*
Synthesizing	Mentoring	Setting-Up
Coordinating	Negotiating	Precision Working
Analyzing	Instructing	Operating-Controlling
Compiling	Supervising	Driving-Operating
Computing	Diverting	Manipulating
Copying	Persuading	Tending
Comparing	Speaking-Signaling	Feeding-Off bearing
No Significant	Serving	Handling
Relationsship	Taking Instructions —	(NSR)
(NSR)	Helping	
	(NSR)	

Each of these relationships has a specific definition and the less obvious of these are given here:

Data (Ideas): Information, knowledge, and conceptions, related to data, people or things, obtained by observation, investigation, interpretation, visualization, mental creation; incapable of being touched; written data take the form of numbers, words, symbols; other data are ideas, concepts, oral verbalization.

---

1. *Dictionary of Occupational Titles.* Fourth edition, 1977. Washington, D.C., U. S. Government Printing Office. Pages 1369-1371.

Synthesizing: Integrating analyses of data to discover facts and/or develop knowledge, concepts, or interpretations.

Coordinating: Determining time, place, and sequence of operations or action to be taken on the basis of analysis of data; executing determinations and/or reporting on events.

Analyzing: Examining and evaluating data. Presenting alternative actions in relation to the evaluation is frequently involved.

Compiling: Gathering, collating, or classifying information about data, people, or things. Reporting and/or carrying out a prescribed action in relation to the information is frequently involved.

Computing: Performing arithmetic operations and reporting on and/or carrying out a prescribed action in relation to them. Does not include counting.

People: Human beings; also animals dealt with on an individual basis as if they were human.

Mentoring: Dealing with individuals in terms of their total personality in order to advise, counsel, and/or guide them with regard to problems that may be resolved by legal, scientific, clinical, spiritual, and/or other professional principles.

Negotiating: Exchanging ideas, information, and opinions with others to formulate policies and programs and/or arrive jointly at decisions, conclusions, or solutions.

Instructing: Teaching subject matter to others, or training others (including animals) through explanation, demonstration, and supervised practice; or making recommendations on the basis of technical disciplines.

Supervising: Determining or interpreting work procedures for a group of workers, assigning specific duties to them, maintaining harmonious relations among them, and promoting efficiency.

Diverting: Amusing others.

Persuading: Influencing others in favor of a product, service, or point of view.

Things: Inanimate objects as distinguished from human beings; substances or materials; machines, tools, equipment; products. A thing is tangible and has shape, form, and other physical characteristics.

Setting Up: Adjusting machines or equipment by replacing or altering tools, jigs, fixtures, and attachments to prepare them to perform their functions, change their performance, or restore their proper functioning if they break down. Workers who set up one or a number of machines for other workers or who set up and personally operate a variety of machines are included here.

Precision Working: Using body members and/or tools or work aids to work, move, guide, or place objects or materials in situations where ultimate responsibility for the attainment of standards occurs and selection of appropriate tools, objects, or materials, and the adjustment of the tool to the task require exercise of considerable judgment.

Handling: Using body members, handtools, and/or special devices to work, move, or carry objects or materials. Involves little or no latitude for judgment with regard to attainment of standards or in selecting tool, object, or material.

A number of different jobs performed in a number of distinct settings may require the same highest functions, and yet may lead to the satisfaction of different values. By stating each of the three hierarchy levels for a job, we establish a sort of role profile for it. If we take a role profile of: coordinating data, mentoring people, NSR things, we will find these roles/levels are demanded by the following occupations (among others): guidance and counseling (educational, psychological, ministerial, social work); legal and related work (lawyer, judge); and medical, veterinary, and related services. All these occupational groups require — at the highest level — coordinating data and mentoring people.

If we go merely one level lower in the hierarchy of function with regard to people (i.e., to negotiating) we now include a whole range of occupations in business administration.

In considering, within a framework of self-awareness, the possible groups of occupations which you may find interesting, rewarding and hopefully open to entry, you must seek current information. Need and demand are not the same. At this writing, there is clear evidence of substantial need for persons in the field of social work beneath the level of the M.S.W. However, budgets, professional vested interests and unresponsive civil service structures hold back the generation of a demand for the baccalaureate degree holder in social work. It is entirely possible though that by the time present freshmen graduate, the demand may exist. Current projections of smaller college enrollments for the next decade almost guarantee a favorable market for *qualified* graduates from 1985 to the end of this century.

Each person must establish her/his own values, but it may be helpful to have some idea of role level in various occupational areas. The following tables are derived from the *Dictionary of Occupational Titles* and give only general occupational titles. Within an occupational group, each person should seek further information from his/her instructor, or pursue the sources of information listed.

While the following tables deal with a wide range of job groups which commonly require or utilize some amount of community college, technical institute, college, or university study, there are many areas which are not included and many details lacking. These can and should be researched by the student with the assistance of the instructor who has familiarity with local and regional opportunities. A complete listing of the physical, biological or social sciences would alone require several pages. Much useful information might be garnered from a university catalog.

HIGHEST ROLE LEVELS – EDUCATIONAL REQUIREMENTS – SOURCES OF INFORMATION in SELECTED OCCUPATIONS

Occupational Group	Highest Function Involved*			Means of Entry	Sources of Information
	Data	People	Things		
ART					
Instructive work, fine arts, theater, music and related fields	synth	instr	NSR	College, university, specialized schools; informal apprenticeship	▪ American Alliance for Health, Physical Education & Recreation, 1201 16th St., NW, Washington, DC 20036 ▪ National Association of Schools of Music, 11250 Roger Bacon Drive, Reston, VA 20090
Instructing others in principles, techniques, application of some form of creative expression; e.g., art, music, dramatics, dance. General or specific instruction. Specific instruction involves evolution of a personal interpretation and application of personal viewpoint to learning processes, development and/or performances of others. Requires: perception for detail, aesthetic appreciation; creativity and imagination; ability to relate to people and communicate ideas; a feeling for form, color, composition.					
DECORATING AND ART WORK	synth	supv pers spk–signl	NSR	Accredited art school or college; sometimes part-time courses	▪ National Art Education Association, 1916 Association Drive, Reston, VA 22091 ▪ American Society of Interior Design, 730 5th Ave., New York, NY 10019
Determining and executing arrangements of objects or materials to produce artistic or decorative effects for apparel, interiors, advertising layouts, motion picture sets, etc.; consultation with customers to contract for services, with salesmen to purchase materials; supervision of others in execution of assignments. Requires: aesthetic appreciation, creative imagination, manual and finger dexterity, eye-hand coordination, ability to communicate ideas and influence others, feeling for spatial relationships and color combinations and supervisory capabilities.					
ART WORK	synth	NSR	prec wk	Vocational high schools, art schools	▪ Industrial Designers Society of America, 1750 Old Meadow Rd., McLean, VA 22101
Creative expression of ideas, feelings, moods in artistic designs, objects, arrangements. Fine arts involve creation and execution of portraits, sculpture, ceramics, mosaics, murals, etc., for their own sake with the artist free to choose media and technique. Commercial arts are concerned with creation and reproduction of commercial and industrial designs involving adherence to technical requirements or functional limitations specified by client or employer. Requires: aesthetic appreciation, creative imagination, artistic judgment concerning harmony of color and line, eye-hand coordination, finger and manual dexterity to paint, draw, use handtools with plaster, clay, stone and other materials; perception of form and design; color discrimination to perceive differences in hue, shade and value; spatial aptitude to visualize and depict three dimensional objects and arrangements on two-dimensional surfaces.					

*See "Hierarchy of Job Relations" on page 33 for key to abbreviations.

Occupational Group	Highest Function Involved*			Means of Entry	Sources of Information
	Data	People	Things		
BUSINESS RELATIONS					
ADMINISTRATION	coord	negot spk-signl	NSR	College graduate formal training	Personnel depts. of large corps., senior placement offices of colleges and universities, also faculties. (The D.O.T. lists 140 separate occupational titles in this group.)
Formulating and carrying out administrative principles, practices, techniques in an organization or establishment; program planning, allocation of responsibilities to organizational components, monitoring the internal activities of these components, coordinating achievements for overall success. Requires: ability to plan, formulate and execute policies and programs; capacity to acquire knowledge of various administrative concepts and practices and apply them to different organizational environments; verbal facility to deal with persons at all levels; facility with numbers to prepare and review various financial and materiel reports; ability to relate to people in a manner to win confidence and establish rapport; flexibility to adjust to changing conditions; an analytical mind to solve complex problems.					
CONTRACT NEGOTIATION AND RELATED WORK	coord	negot spk-signl	NSR	Law study often required; in-field experience important; not usually entered directly from college	▪ American Society for Personnel Administration, 30 Park Drive, Berea, OH 44017
Representing and promoting the interests of one or more individuals or an organization in negotiations or discussions concerned with the exchange of money for products, property or services; or with passage of legislation affecting a client's welfare. Requires: liking for public contact work; ability to understand contract and property laws, legal and insurance terminology; reading comprehension and conversational agility; persuasive powers; sensitivity to attitudes and reactions of others.					
BUSINESS TRAINING	analyz	instr	NSR	Personnel courses, teaching methods; in-field experience	▪ American Society for Personnel Administration. (See address above.)
Providing general training and orientation to new employees in a business or commercial environment — company organization and policy, personnel regulations, company operating procedures, terminology, customer relations. Requires: interest in people and ability to communicate ideas.					
SUPERVISORY WORK (clerical, sales, etc.)	coord	supv	NSR	Supervisory practice courses – usual promotion from inside	Employers in specific fields
Supervising and coordinating activities of personnel engaged in clerical, sales and related work. Requires: ability to become familiar with one or more clerical or sales activity; verbal ability; clerical aptitude; ability to motivate people to work cooperatively.					
MANAGERIAL WORK	coord	spk-signl	NSR	Usually bus. admin. grads. of colleges management trainee	Same as for Administration. (The D.O.T. lists approximately 280 separate occupational titles in this group.)
Organizing and coordinating functions of a unit, department or branch of an organization or establishment; planning and coordination of a singular program project or other organized endeavor, public or private, for a specific purpose. Requires: ability to plan, initiate, execute programs; ability to understand, interpret, apply procedures and directives; numerical facility to analyze and use statistics, maintain production and inventory controls and records; leadership qualities; verbal facility; ability to relate to people in order to motivate and direct employees, maintain good employer-employee and customer relationships.					

*See "Hierarchy of Job Relations" on page 33 for key to abbreviations.

Occupational Group	Highest Function Involved*			Means of Entry	Sources of Information
	Data	People	Things		
BUSINESS RELATIONS – continued **CONSULTATIVE & BUSINESS SERVICES** Examining methods, procedures, problems in clerical, statistical, budgetary, organizational and similar areas of concern and recommending improvements or solutions; consult with clients; conduct research to amass complete details; evaluate the situation and present recommendations; frequently implement the suggestions and findings. Requires: capacity to learn and apply principles and techniques involved in subject matter areas; verbal facility and ability to relate to people in consultation or gathering of information; numerical ability for dealing with statistical and budgetary matters; attention to detail and clerical perception for examining records and preparing reports; ability to adjust to different environments and grasp varying concepts and procedures; organizational ability.	coord analyz	speaking signaling	NSR	College graduate training program or equivalent experience	■ American Management Association, 135 W. 50th St., New York, NY 10020
ACCOUNTING, AUDITING and RELATED WORK Devising accounting systems and procedures; appraising assets and evaluating costing methods, investment programs, monetary risks and rates; preparing statistical tabulations and diagrams, financial reports, statements and schedules for use by management. Requires: ability to concentrate for long periods; good vocabulary and verbal expression; organizational ability, speed and accuracy in making numerical determinations; memory for detail; ability to understand principles of accounting, statistics and fiscal management.	coord analyz	NSR	NSR	Bachelor's degree with course emphasis	■ National Association of Accountants, 919 3rd Ave., New York, NY 10022 ■ American Institute of Certified Public Accountants, 1211 Ave. of the Americas, New York, NY 10030
INTERVIEWING, INFORMATION GIVING Interviewing individuals to gather pertinent information, evaluate information and/or the individual's qualifications for a variety of considerations; dispensing information usually relative to correct interpretation of rules and regulations governing insurance, education, housing, etc. Requires: verbal facility; numerical ability and clerical perception; ability to reason analytically; neat appearance, poise, composure.	coord analyz	speaking signaling	NSR	College graduate, courses in applied psychology, sociology; personnel related	See Business training and education. ■ American Society for Personnel Administration, 30 Park Drive, Berea, OH 44107
TITLE and CONTRACT SEARCH and ANALYSIS Examining, authenticating and preparing such legal and business documents as titles, contracts, mortgages and liens. Requires: ability to acquire the necessary understanding of official or legal business terminology and documentary regulations; organizational and analytical ability for scanning documents, deriving pertinent points, recording conclusions; good reading comprehension and speed.	coord analyz	NSR	NSR	Law or business administration	■ Commercial Law League of America, 222 W. Adams St., Chicago, IL 60606

*See "Hierarchy of Job Relations" on page 33 for key to abbreviations.

Occupational Group	Highest Function Involved*			Means of Entry	Sources of Information
	Data	People	Things		
COUNSELING, GUIDANCE and SOCIAL WORK SOCIAL SCIENCE, PSYCHOLOGICAL and RELATED RESEARCH	synth	NSR	NSR	Master's degree, working toward Ph.D. if educationally oriented	▪ American Sociological Association, 1722 N St., NW, Washington, DC 20036 ▪ American Psychological Association, 1200 17th St., NW, Washington, DC 20036
GUIDANCE and COUNSELING (also Ministerial Work)	coord analyz	mentor	NSR	Bachelor's degree M.S.W. commonly in social work and M.Ed. in school counseling	▪ National Association of Social Workers, 1425 H St., NW, Washington, DC 20005 ▪ National Vocational Guidance Association (and other divisions of American Personnel & Guidance Association) 2 Skyline Place, Suite 400, 520 Leesburg Pike, Falls Church, VA 22041
EDUCATION and TRAINING SUPERVISORY and INSTRUCTIVE WORK (Nursing and Related Services)	coord	instr	NSR	Associate or bachelor's degree plus experience in field	▪ American Society for Medical Technology, 5555 W. Loop, So., Suite 200, Bellaire, TX 77401 ▪ American Dietetic Association, 430 N. Michigan Ave., Chicago, IL 60611 ▪ American Public Health Association, Inc., 1015 18th St., NW, Washington, DC 20036 ▪ National League for Nursing, 10 Columbus Circle, New York, NY 10019

Investigation into governments, ethnic groups, social units, cultures, languages, economic conditions, other elements of society, and into various aspects of the individual human being (intelligence, socialization, personality, emotionality or industrial efficiency); collecting, evaluating and interpreting data, formulating, devising or developing original theories, methods, procedures or techniques aimed at solving theoretical or practical problems or adding enlightenment to specific areas of knowledge, communicating the findings and conclusions of research endeavors through reports, publications and other media. Requires: intelligence to understand principles, laws and methods of investigation; lucidity in expression; organizational ability; high degree of rationality; inventiveness; analytical ability; sometimes an understanding of methods of statistical or mathematical analysis.

Guiding and/or counseling individuals or groups in solution of occupational, educational, personal or social problems; e.g., assisting prison parolees in gaining employment and adjusting to society; counseling high school students about college admission requirements and curricula; counseling unhappy or frustrated workers or jobseekers into more fulfilling work; and assisting troubled individuals or families toward normal social adjustment. Requires: sympathetic attitude toward the welfare of others; verbal facility; organizational ability; tact, poise and general demeanor to inspire confidence.

Planning, organizing and conducting educational and training programs in such fields as nursing, dietetics, medical technology or health, supervising personnel in these fields — in a clinic, hospital, school, public or private health agency or industrial organization. Requires: ability to impart knowledge in instructive, advisory, demonstrative or supervisory situation; organizational ability; interest in health and welfare of people.

*See "Hierarchy of Job Relations" on page 33 for key to abbreviations.

Occupational Group	Highest Function Involved*			Means of Entry	Sources of Information
	Data	People	Things		

EDUCATION and TRAINING - continued

INDUSTRIAL TRAINING

| | coord | instr | NSR | Extensive experience; often a college degree | Training departments of industrial employers; sometimes associations in regional areas |

Providing specialized training in proper functioning or execution of machines, equipment, systems, procedures, and/or methods, to new employees, tenure employees or customers. Requires: manual dexterity, eye-hand-foot coordination and spatial ability to demonstrate equipment; interest in communicating ideas; analytical mind.

VOCATIONAL TRAINING

| | coord | instr | NSR | Certification, bachelor's degree min.; also experience | ■ National Education Association of the U.S. 1201 16th St., NW, Washington, DC 20036 |

Teaching, demonstrating, and/or advising others in the productive and efficient utilization of agricultural, home economics and similar vocational principles, subject matter and skills — in a school, industrial, commercial, community or home environment. Requires: interest in people and ability to communicate ideas; intellectual capacity sufficient to acquire necessary background in subject matter and teaching techniques; organizational ability to present facts and plan programs; perception for clerical detail.

FLIGHT and RELATED TRAINING

| | coord analyz | instr | NSR | Extensive experience often F.A.A. pilot license | All major airlines. ■ Air Transport Association of America, 1709 New York Ave., NW, Washington, DC 20006 |

Training and evaluating the proficiency of airplane pilots; teaching flying techniques; giving flying proficiency tests; administering oral and written examinations. Requires: eye-hand-foot coordination, spatial and form perception; mentality and interest sufficient to acquire vocational background, ability to communicate ideas; analytical mind to organize facts and plan programs of instruction

HIGH SCHOOL, COLLEGE, UNIVERSITY and RELATED EDUCATION

| | analyz | instr | NSR | Bachelor's degree student teaching state certification; universities require at least a Master's and often a Ph.D. | ■ American Association of University Professors 1 Dupont Circle, NW, Washington, DC 20036 ■ American Federation of Teachers, 11 Dupont Circle, NW, Washington, DC 20036 ■ National Education Association (address above) ■ U.S. Department of Health, Education & Welfare. (See also State Departments of Education.) |

Teaching academic or commercial subjects which are usually part of an established curriculum in a high school, college or university as a member of the staff. Tutoring individuals or groups in either academic or non-academic environment is occasionally involved. Requires: Interest in people; ability to communicate ideas; intellectual capacity to acquire background in subject area and teaching techniques; organizational ability to present facts and plan programs; perception for clerical detail.

KINDERGARTEN, ELEMENTARY SCHOOL, etc.

| | analyz | instr | NSR | State certification Bachelor's degree in most states | |

Requires: interest in working with children, ability to communicate; organizational ability; arithmetic ability; perception for clerical detail.

*See "Hierarchy of Job Relations" on page 33 for key to abbreviations.

Occupational Group	Highest Function Involved*			Means of Entry	Sources of Information
	Data	People	Things		

EDUCATION and TRAINING — continued

PHYSICAL EDUCATION

| | analyz | instr | NSR | Bachelor's degree state certification often master's | ■ American Alliance for Health, Physical Education & Recreation, 1201 16th St., NW, Washington, DC 20036 |

Instructing others in principles of physical development, techniques for utilizing specialized skills in swimming, boxing, gymnastics, other sports; conducting physical training and sports programs for schools, camps, playgrounds; evaluating abilities of students in relation to course or activity, determining best training methods. Requires: organizational ability to plan for and/or officiate in games and competitions; ability to deal with varied personalities; manual and finger dexterity; eye-hand-foot coordination; verbal ability; physical strength, agility or stamina.

TRAINING SERVICES

| | analyz | instr | NSR | Often personnel background | ■ American Society for Personnel Administration, 30 Park Drive, Berea, OH 44017 |

Providing orientation and training in performance fundamentals to both new and regular employees of an organization; following up initial training with progress observations and testing in order to improve level of performance standards. Activities involve use of lectures, visual aids, demonstrations, and evaluation of trainee comprehension. Requires: interest in communicating ideas; analytical ability to organize facts and plan programs of instruction.

ANIMAL TRAINING

| | analyz compil | instr | NSR | Experience; in some cases advanced study in behavioral sciences | ■ American Society of Animal Science, c/o Claude Cruse, 113 N. Neil St., Rm. 425, Champaign, IL 61820 |

Training animals for a variety of purposes: to perform in amusement events; disciplining domestic animals; training dogs to serve as guides for blind or as guards. Requires: liking animals; ability to understand the behavior and reaction of animals; finger and hand dexterity; motor coordination; eye-hand-foot coordination; physical stamina; interest in outdoor work.

ENGINEERING

ENGINEERING RESEARCH and DESIGN

| | synth | NSR | prec wk | Usually at least a Bachelor's degree; advanced degree | ■ Engineers' Council for Professional Development, 345 E. 47th St., New York, NY 10017
■ National Society of Professional Engineers, 2029 K St., NW, Washington, DC 20006
■ American Institute of Aeronautics & Astronautics, 1290 Ave. of Americas, New York, NY 10019 |

Using and adapting earth substances, properties of matter, natural sources of power and physical forces to satisfy human needs and desires: conducting analyses and experiments of materials and systems by application of known laws and relationships; conceiving and designing new structures, machines, tools, precision instruments and other devices. Requires: good visual acuity, creative talent or imagination; ability to perceive or visualize spatial relationships of plane and solid objects; logical mind; organizational ability; facility in mathematics.

SALES ENGINEERING

| | coord | pers | prec wk | Engineering degree plus some business administration formal training programs | |

Technical presentation, sale and installation of engineering products or services, applied in a market situation: advising and assisting customers in purchasing such commodities and services as industrial machinery, air-conditioning systems, and utilities; modifying or adapting them to suit particular needs of customers; direct installation; close liaison with customers to solve technical problems. Requires: facility with numbers and geometric, arithmetic and algebraic principles; ability to visualize spatial relationships; conversational agility and persuasive powers.

*See "Hierarchy of Job Relations" on page 33 for key to abbreviations.

ENGINEERING — continued

Occupational Group	Highest Function Involved*			Means of Entry	Sources of Information
	Data	People	Things		
ENGINEERING, SCIENTIFIC and TECHNICAL COORDINATION Planning and coordinating engineering, scientific and technical programs and activities in a scientific or industrial environment; formulating policies and standards, planning and directing projects and programs, monitoring personnel. Requires: organizational ability to plan, formulate, carry out programs and policies; verbal facility to deal with personnel; mathematical ability.	coord	spkg. sgnlg	NSR	Bachelor's degree in specialty; often advanced degree	▪ American Society of Agricultural Engineers, P.O. Box 410, St. Joseph, MI 49085 ▪ Biomedical Engineering Society, 3900 Wisconsin Ave, Washington, DC 20016 ▪ American Ceramic Society, Inc., 65 Ceramic Drive, Columbus, OH 43214 ▪ American Institute of Chemical Engineers, 345 E. 47th St., New York, NY 10017 ▪ American Society of Civil Engineers, 345 E. 47th St., New York, NY 10017
DRAFTING and RELATED WORK Translation of ideas, rough sketches, specifications and calculations of engineers, architects and designers into complete and accurate working plans for use in building or manufacturing. Requires: ability to visualize spatial relationships, perceive slight differences in visual matter and work with detail; finger dexterity.	coord, analyz	NSR	prec wk	Vocational or technical high school, technical institute or community college	
TECHNICAL WORK, ENGINEERING and RELATED FIELDS Application of engineering related and technical knowledge in direct support of the engineer; functional parts of engineering, practical application of fundamental theory in such specialized areas as research, design and development. Requires: ability to learn and apply basic engineering and technical principles and methods; facility with mathematics and language and spatial perception.	coord, analyz	NSR	prec wk	Technical institute or community college	▪ Institute of Electrical & Electronics Engineers, 1111 19th St., NW, Washington, DC 20036 ▪ American Institute of Industrial Engineers, 25 Technology Park/Atlanta, Norcross, GA 30092
ENGINEERING and RELATED WORK Application of engineering knowledge to planning, direction and installation of projects and systems: civil engineering, mechanical engineering, and electrical engineering. Requires: organizational ability; clear verbal expression; ability to learn and apply engineering principles and methods; spatial and form perception; facility with mathematics.	coord, analyz	NSR	hdlg	Usual B.S. in engineering, sometimes advanced degree	▪ American Society of Mechanical Engineers, Inc., 345 E. 47th St., New York, NY 10017
INDUSTRIAL ENGINEERING and RELATED WORK Applying a knowledge of industrial organization and processes to insure efficient utilization of machines, materials and manpower: time, motion and incentive studies; procedures and methods planning; cost control; safety planning; plant layout; operations research. Requires: ability to learn and apply engineering principles and methods, organizational ability, facility with mathematics, clear verbal expression, ability to perceive or envision relative paths or positions of stationary and moving objects.	coord, analyz	NSR	NSR	Bachelor's degree in engineering	▪ American Institute of Mining, Metallurgical & Petroleum Engineers, 345 E. 37th St., New York, NY 10017
SURVEYING, PROSPECTING and RELATED WORK Requires: understanding of principles of geometry and trigonometry, strong liking for outdoor work, ability to draw, finger dexterity, good vision and health, physical stamina, ability to perceive relationships of objects in space or to envision objects of two or three dimensions on flat surfaces.	coord, analyz	NSR	NSR	High school plus experience in field; college degree required for professional registration	

*See "Hierarchy of Job Relations" on page 33 for key to abbreviations.

Occupational Group	Highest Function Involved*			Means of Entry	Sources of Information
	Data	People	Things		
ENTERTAINMENT **CREATIVE ENTERTAINMENT WORK: DRAMATICS, INSTRUMENTS and VOCAL MUSICAL WORK, RHYTHMICS**	synth	divert	NSR	Historically by persistence, informal apprenticeship; increasingly special schools, colleges and universities integrate music, dance, etc., with psychiatric social activity	▪ National Association of Schools of Music, 11250 Roger Bacon Dr., Reston, VA 20090 ▪ American Guild of Musical Artists, Inc., 1841 Broadway, NY 10023 ▪ National Repertory Theatre Foundation, 35 Beekman Place, New York, NY 10022 ▪ American Theatre Association, 1000 Vermont Ave., NW, Washington, DC 20005

Entertaining others by creating and perfecting original acts or by interpreting and presenting stock routines in an original manner; work is highly imaginative. Requires: creative imagination facility with language, retentive memory, ability to understand people and adapt to different types of audiences, nimbleness in use of fingers, hands and arms in cases where props or movement are important to the performance; poise, and desire for public recognition.

Entertaining others by spoken word and accompanying physical actions; worker must usually go through cycle of auditioning for a role, learning lines, incorporating movement and gestures with dialog, interpreting meaning of a role under guidance of a director in rehearsals, adding costumes and makeup, performing before an audience — live in a theater, before television or motion picture cameras or a combination thereof. Requires: facility with language, creative imagination, retentive memory, poise, ability to adapt to fluctuating situations.

Entertaining others by music (instrumental or vocal) or dance (rhythmics) requires ability to complete intensive training, creativity, ability to recognize and remember musical notes and symbols, motor coordination (verbal and language facility for vocal entertaining), good health and physical stamina.

Occupational Group	Data	People	Things	Means of Entry	Sources of Information
RADIO ANNOUNCING and RELATED WORK	coord analyz	divert spk-signl	NSR	Specialized schools; some college programs; first class radio tel. license	▪ National Association of Broadcasters, 1771 N St., NW, Washington, DC 20036

Introducing radio and television programs and segments thereof; acting as master of ceremonies for banquets or similar occasions; verbally translating speech from one language to another; giving running commentaries or descriptions of live-action events. Workers either read from a prepared script, present memorized material or speak extemporaneously. Requires: facility with language, good vocabulary, originality and inventiveness when speaking extemporaneously; ability to relate to an audience, seen or unseen; pleasant speaking voice with good diction, good memory.

Occupational Group	Data	People	Things	Means of Entry	Sources of Information
FARMING, FISHING and FORESTRY **TECHNICAL WORK, SCIENCE and RELATED FIELDS**	compil	NSR	manip	High school and post high school science courses, especially laboratory practice	▪ Society of American Foresters, 5400 Grosvenor Lane, Washington, DC 20014

Applying basic scientific knowledge to performance of a variety of supporting tasks in a laboratory or similar scientific environment. Requires: ability to absorb technical information and follow established procedures; verbal ability to learn and use technical terminology; ability to perceive minute differences in forms and compositional characteristics; manual dexterity; capacity to pay strict attention to detail in work of a closely prescribed and organized nature.

*See "Hierarchy of Job Relations" on page 33 for key to abbreviations.

Occupational Group	Highest Function Involved*			Means of Entry	Sources of Information
	Data	People	Things		

INVESTIGATING, INSPECTING and TESTING

INVESTIGATING, PROTECTING, etc.

	Data	People	Things	Means of Entry	Sources of Information
	coord analyz	spkg signl	NSR	High school; increasingly some college; extensive formal job training	Federal, state, local or private agencies of interest

Conducting investigations and examinations designed to determine compliance with statutes, ordinances and similar regulations affecting the public interest; enforcing laws or regulations to protect citizenry from harm. Requires: capacity to acquire knowledge of laws and regulations and learn investigative procedures and methods; verbal ability; tact and diplomacy; ability to perform under stress in face of danger or resistance; organizational ability in order to gather and evaluate facts; self-confidence; physical stamina.

MATERIALS ANALYSIS and RELATED WORK

	Data	People	Things	Means of Entry	Sources of Information
	coord analyz compil	NSR	prec wk	Sometimes bachelor's degree; extensive experience	■ National Bureau of Standards, Washington, DC 20234

Applying principles of chemistry, physics, metallurgy and related disciplines to analysis, testing and compounding of such materials as ores, foods, chemicals and drugs; activities range from food tasting to objective evaluation of test data on properties such as fuels, gems and textiles. Requires: attention to detail; facility with mathematics; form perception to recognize physical differences in materials.

APPRAISING and INVESTIGATIVE WORK

	Data	People	Things	Means of Entry	Sources of Information
	coord analyz	NSR	manip hdlg	Experience; community college helpful (tech)	■ American Society of Appraisers, P.O. Box 17265, Washington, DC 20041

Applying a knowledge of principles and techniques pertinent to fields such as mining, construction, merchandising, sanitation to investigate condition or state of objects, systems, activities and procedures; also verifying compliance with laws and standards and recommending remedial action. Requires: numerical skill to apply mathematics to investigation of specific situations; spatial aptitude to visualize three-dimensional forms and relationships as represented in blueprints; form perception to distinguish details in objects or drawings.

LAW and LAW ENFORCEMENT

LEGAL and RELATED WORK

	Data	People	Things	Means of Entry	Sources of Information
	coord	mentor negot	NSR	Law school, pass written test for admission to bar	■ American Bar Association, 1155 E. 60th St., Chicago, IL 60637 ■ Association of American Law Schools, Suite 370, 1 Dupont Circle, NW, Washington, DC 20036

Applying a knowledge of municipal, county, state or federal laws to various phases of litigating and adjudicating; advising clients of legal rights, representing them in courts of law when necessary; preparing legal documents; investigating and adjusting claims for damages and suits; negotiating settlements out of court and representing clients before quasi-judicial or administrative agencies of government; acting as trustees, guardians or executors of estates; prosecuting individuals accused of crimes. Requires: facility with language, ability to relate to people, originality and persuasiveness; unwavering accuracy for complex detailed work.

*See "Hierarchy of Job Relations" on page 33 for key to abbreviations.

Occupational Group	Highest Function Involved* Data	People	Things	Means of Entry	Sources of Information
LAW and LAW ENFORCEMENT – Continued **PROTECTING and RELATED WORK** Rendering services designed to defend the person, property or rights of individuals, establishments or general public against injury, loss or disturbance resulting from criminal or disorderly acts, unwanted intrusion, accidents, fire or other hazards. Requires: ability to exercise initiative in relating to people and adjusting to fluctuating situations; equanimity in face of danger or resistance; manual dexterity and motor coordination for using firearms; honesty and dependability; physical stamina.	analyz compil	spk-sgnl serving	NSR	High school, written test common; increasingly college or community college and university study a requirement	Federal, state or local agencies. ■ International Association of Chiefs of Police, 11 Firstfield Rd., Gaithersburg, MD 20760 ■ International Association of Fire Chiefs, 1329 18th St., NW, Washington, DC 20036
MANAGERIAL and SUPERVISORY WORK **SUPERVISORY WORK** Supervising and coordinating activities of personnel engaged in serving or performing services for others. Requires: ability to become familiar with one or more service activities; plan and direct activities, communicate effectively with superiors and subordinates, prepare written reports, compute quantities and costs of supplies; clerical perception to detect errors in records; ability to motivate people and train new employees.	coord	supv	NSR	Experience; special schools – hotel and restaurant management, cooking, etc.	■ American Hotel & Motel Association, 888 Seventh Ave., New York, NY 10019
MATHEMATICS and SCIENCE **HEALTH PHYSICS** Conducting research, devising and monitoring training programs to protect plant and laboratory workers from health hazards such as radiation. Requires: thoroughness and penchant for detail, inquisitive mind and fertile imagination, ability to perceive minute differences in forms and compositional characteristics.	synth	instr	prec wk	Graduate degree in physics	■ U.S. Atomic Energy Commission, Washington, DC 20545
SCIENTIFIC RESEARCH; MATHEMATICS and PHYSICAL SCIENCES, Etc. Applying principles of chemistry, physics, metallurgy and astronomy to: basic research designed to increase man's knowledge of the properties of matter and energy; applied research designed to utilize knowledge gained from basic research to develop new products and processes; and solution of practical scientific problems. Requires: thoroughness, penchant for detail, facility with mathematics. Investigation into atmospheric, astronomical, geographical phenomena and conditions, theoretical aspects of physics and mathematics, automatic data processing systems and programs. Requires: ability to understand basic laws of nature and scientific methods of investigation; inventiveness; ability to represent and relate abstract ideas by means of symbols; organizational ability; retentive memory; clerical perception; lucid verbal expression; ability to envision or perceive relative paths or positions of stationary and moving objects; ability to grasp mathematical and statistical concepts.	synth coord	NSR	prec wk	Bachelor's/master's degree in specialty; B.S. or M.S. often enough for statistical analytical math fields; M.S. required for more responsible work; Ph.D. in process	Associations or societies within specific disciplines

*See "Hierarchy of Job Relations" on page 33 for key to abbreviations.

Occupational Group	Highest Function Involved*			Means of Entry	Sources of Information
	Data	People	Things		
MEDICINE and HEALTH **SURGERY** Diagnosis and treatment of human disease, injury, deformity by manual or instrumental operations. Requires: spatial perception to visualize position and arrangement of unseen organs, bony structures, body tissue from X-ray photographs and knowledge of anatomy; form perception to see details in body tissues and structures; combination of finger and manual dexterity and motor coordination to use surgical instruments with precision and speed; ability to make quick decisions and perform difficult tasks under stress; stamina to maintain high level of concentration, alertness and performance during prolonged periods.	coord	mentor	prec wk	Pre-med and medical study 8-9 years plus 3-6 years of advanced training; licensure exam in all states; professional examining board highly selective.	See next chapter under medical and associated occupations. ▪ American College of Surgeons, 55 E. Erie St., Chicago, IL 60611 ▪ American Medical Association, 535 N. Dearborn St., Chicago, IL 60610
MEDICAL, VETERINARY and RELATED SERVICES Applying medical science to diagnosis, prevention and treatment of human and animal diseases, disorders and injuries. Requires spatial perception to visualize position and arrangement of unseen organs, bony structures and tissues from X-ray photographs and knowledge of anatomy; numerical ability for study of chemistry, physics, calculus and other basic subjects; form perception to observe physical manifestations of disease or tissue damage; stamina to work long and irregular hours when required; finger dexterity for administering injections and performing autopsies.	coord	mentor	NSR	Pre-med and med study 7-8 years, 1 year internship min. for M.D.; 6-7 years for dentistry or vet. medicine; legal and/or professional certification	▪ American Medical Association. (See above.) ▪ American Academy of Family Physicians, 1740 W. 92nd St., Kansas City, MO 64114 ▪ American Veterinary Medical Association, 930 N. Meacham Rd., Schaumburg, IL 60193
THERAPEUTIC and RELATED WORK Planning, organizing, directing and participating in recreational, educational vocational and social programs designed to aid in rehabilitation of physically or mentally ill or handicapped. Requires: ability to comprehend such subjects as psychology, anatomy, physiology, and to achieve empathy and rapport with physically disabled and mentally ill people; ability to exercise necessary craft or artistic skills.	coord	instr	NSR	Bachelor's degree in specialty; legal or professional certification	▪ American Physical Therapy Association, 1156 15th St., NW, Washington, DC 20005 ▪ National Association of Physical Therapists, P.O. Box 367, W. Covina, CA 91793
NURSING, X-RAY and RELATED SERVICES Caring for sick and injured, providing nursing services for prevention of illness and promotion of good health; utilizing X-ray and other medical laboratory equipment for diagnostic and therapeutic purposes. Requires: facility for relating to people, interest in their welfare; exactness and precision for preparing or administering treatment or medication, keeping charts; ability to perceive differences in anatomical components; finger dexterity and eye-hand coordination; cleanliness, good health, freedom from communicable diseases.	compil	spk-sgnl	NSR	2-5 years depending on program includes supervised practice professional and/or legal certification or licensure	▪ American Nurses Association, Inc., 2420 Pershing Rd., Kansas City, MO 64108 ▪ Association of Operating Room Nurses, Inc., 10170 E. Miss. Ave., Denver, CO 80231 ▪ International Society for Clinical Laboratory Technology, 818 Olive St., Suite 918, St. Louis, MO 63101

*See "Hierarchy of Job Relations" on page 33 for key to abbreviations.

Occupational Group	Highest Function Involved*			Means of Entry	Sources of Information
	Data	People	Things		

MERCHANDISING

PROMOTION and PUBLICITY — Data: synth, People: spkg, Things: NSR

Means of Entry: Often liberal arts background plus courses or experience in sales, journalism, etc. Highly competitive

Sources of Information: ▪ Public Relations Society of America, Inc., 845 3rd Ave., New York, NY 10022

Planning, directing, conducting advertising and public relations programs designed to promote the sale of products and services, create good will and/or establish a favorable image. Requires: verbal facility, originality to develop practical approaches to unique problems, self-confidence and initiative to assume responsibility, perseverance to deal with problems involving persistent frustrations, persuasiveness to deal with people in competitive situations.

PURCHASE and SALES WORK — Data: coord, People: persuad, Things: NSR

Means of Entry: Bachelor's degree, usually in business administration, formal training programs

Sources of Information: ▪ Sales & Marketing Executives International, 380 Lexington Ave., New York, NY 10017

Applying a knowledge of contracts, credit and marketing conditions, sales methods to a merchandising situation; frequently requiring a technical knowledge of materials or products sold. Requires: ability to acquire and apply knowledge of contracts, credit, marketing conditions, sales psychology; ability to relate to people; powers of persuasion; verbal facility; numerical ability in some instances; initiative and drive.

SALES and SERVICE WORK — Data: analyz, People: persuad, Things: prec wk

Means of Entry: Increasingly technical institute or extensive experience; for complex products. Bachelor's degree in science or engineering

Sources of Information:
▪ American Advertising Federation, 1225 Connecticut Ave., NW, Washington, DC 20036
▪ Sales & Marketing Executives International (See address above.)

Selling, installing, servicing machines, equipment and similar products; requires knowledge of composition and functioning of products sold to provide customer with repair, adjustment and similar services. Requires: ability to communicate, to compute costs, prepare estimates; spatial perception to visualize functioning of installed equipment; ability to establish rapport with customers; sufficient understanding of technical data to solve problems; powers of persuasion; finger and hand dexterity.

MUSIC

MUSICAL WORK, CREATIVE — Data: synth, People: NSR, Things: NSR

Means of Entry: College or special school; increasingly graduate courses; talent

Sources of Information: ▪ National Association of Schools of Music, 11250 Roger Bacon Dr., No. 5, Reston, VA 20090

Requires: ability to absorb musical training, understand and apply principles of music; creative imagination and aesthetic appreciation; verbal facility when music and verse are used together or where music reflects a story; ability to perceive differences in shapes and forms in order to read and score music; tonal memory; a feeling for rhythm and melody; good hearing.

RADIO and TELEVISION TRANSMITTING — Data: analyz, People: NSR, Things: operat

Means of Entry: Technical institute; community college; often college (engineering); F.C.C. licensure

Sources of Information: *See "Hierarchy of Job Relations" on page 33 for key to abbreviations.

Setting up and operating radio and television transmitting, receiving and studio-control equipment in fixed and mobile stations; setting up and operating electronic control equipment to mix and control sound for transmission over closed circuit systems or to record programs on disc, tape or film. Requires: ability to learn codes and technical terminology, ability to work skilfully with hands installing and adjusting radio and TV equipment, ability to maintain attention to detail.

WRITING

Occupational Group	Highest Function Involved*			Means of Entry	Sources of Information
	Data	People	Things		
JOURNALISM and EDITORIAL WORK Writing or editing material designed to induce specific actions, attitudes or opinions; editing material designed to inform or amuse the public; directing the policy and production of a publication or similar medium of communication or department thereof; sometimes supervisory. Requires: facility with language and good vocabulary; originality and inventiveness; ability to understand and relate to people; organizational ability; powers of persuasion; attention to detail.	synth	negot	NSR	Experience; increasingly some college study, specialized courses	See next chapter under Journalism and Communications ■ National Conference of Editorial Writers, 1725 N St., NW, Washington, DC 20036
CREATIVE WRITING Expressing ideas, feelings and personal interpretations by means of the written word; writing poetry, fiction, criticism, lyrics, advertising copy, and dramatic works. Requires: understanding of concepts related to theme, character, plot, tone; creativity and imagination; extensive vocabulary; ability to read analytically; sense of rhythm and euphony; retentive memory; ability to identify oneself with others and their experiences; lucidity of expression.	synth	NSR	NSR	Impossible to define but journalism, literature, subject matter background, history, etc., useful	■ Authors League of America, 234 W. 44th St., New York, NY 10036 ■ Writers Guild of America—East, 22 W. 48th St., New York, NY 10036 ■ Writers Guild of America—West, 8955 Beverly Blvd., Los Angeles, CA 90048
TECHNICAL WRITING and RELATED WORK Preparing written descriptions of technical operations and developments, kinds and uses of industrial property, structural and functional relationships of machines and equipment; collecting information by observing industrial activities, interviewing supervisory and technical personnel, reading or studying engineering drawings, journals, manuals and other technical materials; revising and correcting previously prepared written materials; describing new or improved work methods, processes, standards and workpieces; writing service manuals, bulletins, articles, other technical publications. Requires: ability to grasp technical subject matter and terminology, lucid verbal expression, ability to visualize spatial relationships of objects on flat surfaces, analytical ability and logic in organizing material.	coord analyz	NSR	NSR	Journalism, English degree with scientific subjects; engineering degree with competence in writing	■ Society for Technical Communication, 815 15th St., NW, Suite 506, Washington, DC 20005
TRANSLATING, EDITING and RELATED WORK Translating the written word from one language to another; analyzing coding systems to decode messages; determining suitability of material for publication; editing material for format, style, grammar, content, composition; conducting research in museums, libraries and archives. Requires: good vocabulary and facility with language; ability to communicate ideas, proper syntax of language being translated; accuracy and precision in editing material; analytical ability to conduct research, abstract pertinent material and prepare clear, concise reports.	analyz	NSR	NSR	College level language study and related English/journalism	■ American Translators Association, P.O. Box 129, Croton-on-Hudson, NY 10520

*See "Hierarchy of Job Relations" on page 33 for key to abbreviations.

Chapter Four

OCCUPATIONAL REGULATION AND GRADUATE STUDY

by

Philip W. Dunphy

Many, and increasingly more occupations are regulated in one way or another. In some of the occupational groups—called professions—self-regulation is a part of the nature of the occupation itself. A profession is, in essence, an occupation dealing with people, at a high level of responsibility and confidence, requiring significant intellectual and emotional development, and a process of education and training often beyond the baccalaureate level, and involving the practitioners in the responsibility of setting standards of education, training, competence and ethical behavior.

The basic professions are the ministry, law, medicine and social work. In all of these fields most recognized practitioners must satisfy requirements of professional associations (not always formal) in order to be allowed to practice, at least in the conventional way. Generally, but not universally, acceptance by the appropriate professional society amounts to acceptance by other regulatory agencies when they exist.

Less clear-cut, still emerging self-regulated fields include architecture, education and engineering. In these and the preceding fields, the general educational background of a member of the occupation is fairly well defined. In most fields, a formal examination of some sort is required of candidates and is administered by the profession itself or by professionals under the supervision of a state government. When state licensure through examination is required, commonly (but not always) the professional recognition—through membership in an appropriate society—is more difficult to achieve than licensure.

In seeking entry to these professional fields, the student should be aware of the appropriate professional society and the requirements of membership. Most commonly, the simplest requirement is that the profession, through some membership group accredits, approves, or otherwise determines the fitness of undergraduate and/or graduate schools which will prepare a candidate for practice. Often, graduates of colleges which do not meet accreditation requirements may not even undertake qualifying examinations or will not be accepted as professional members. In those cases where a college fails to receive, or loses accreditation, the program or college is usually closed. The most stringent regulation is within the fields of law and medicine—in each of which it is virtually impossible to be allowed to practice unless a candidate graduates from an accredited graduate school and passes qualifying examinations.

The following general information on these fields will be of help to you in planning your appropriate course of action: (These professions all require accreditation or licensure).

Law:

Schools or colleges of law are approved by The American Bar Association (A.B.A.), 1155 East 60th Street, Chicago, IL 60637 and/or The Association of American Law Schools (A.A.L.S.), One Dupont Circle, NW, Washington, DC 20036. Admission to approved schools usually requires completion of the Law School Admission Test. A few admit at the end of the third year of college. Selectivity varies. Graduates of approved colleges may apply for bar examinations given by states. Successful candidates are admitted to the bar of that state. Admission to practice in other states is fairly routine. The A.A.L.S. annually issues a directory of the accredited law schools; and the A.B.A. list is printed in the fall in *Review of Legal Education.*

Medicine:

Medical colleges are approved by a joint committee representing the American Medical Association (AMA), 535 North Dearborn St., Chicago, IL 60610, and the Association of American Medical Colleges, One Dupont Circle, NW, Washington, DC 20036. Admission to approved colleges is highly selective. All require applicants to complete the Medical College Admission Test. Graduates are required to intern in approved hospitals for at least one year. On successful completion, a doctor may take state qualifying examinations. On successful completion, he is eligible for state licensure. Licensure in other states is fairly routine. To continue in practice and remain a recognized member of the profession, the M.D. must ordinarily maintain additional professional membership in a special or general academy or college *of the profession*—e.g., American Academy of Family Physicians, American College of Surgeons, etc. All specialties require further formal work, supervised practice, and formal examination. The A.A.M.C. issues an annual booklet, *Medical School Admission Requirements, U.S.A. and Canada.* In addition, the Council on Medical Education of the A.M.A. accredits educational programs in eight allied medical services in conjunction with professional organizations in the field. Programs in Cytotechnology, inhalation therapy, medical records technology and X-ray technology are commonly taught in hospitals. The other four areas are:

Medical Record Librarianship—American Medical Record Assn., John Hancock Ctr., 875 N. Michigan Ave., Chicago, IL 60611.

Medical Technology—list available from the American Society for Medical Technologists, Suite 1600, Herman Professional Building, Houston, TX 77025 or the American Medical Technologists, 710 Higgins Rd., Park Ridge, IL 60068.

Occupational Therapy—American Occupational Therapy Association, Inc., Executive Blvd., Suite 200, Rockville, MD 20852; also examines and registers practitioners.

Physical Therapy—American Physical Therapy Association, 1156 15th St., NW, Washington, DC 20008. Practitioners licensed or registered by states.

Other Medical Areas:

Dentistry: Four years beyond entry after two to four years of college. Some pre-dental programs offered by junior colleges. All require the Dental Aptitude Test. Licensed by state based on state examination or National Board of Dental Examiners Test. Accreditation by the Council on Dental Education of the American Dental Association, 211 East Chicago Ave., Chicago, IL 60611.

Dental Hygiene: Also dental assisting and dental laboratory technology. Same accrediting agency as above. Dental hygiene requires two to four years of college, depending on the program. State licensure.

Nursing: Accreditation by the National League for Nursing, 10 Columbus Circle, New York, NY 10019. Licensure by states by examination at Licensed Practical Nurse and Registered Nurse level. Graduate programs in specialties also accredited by NLN. Some diploma programs offered by hospitals. Graduates of non-NLN programs may apply for examination in most states.

Optometry: Schools are accredited by the Council on Optometric Education, 7000 Chippewa St., St. Louis, MO 63119. Usually a six-year program, last four specific. Information from the American Optometric Association, 7000 Chippewa St., St. Louis, MO 63119.

Osteopathy: Schools are accredited by the American Osteopathic Association, 212 East Ohio Street, Chicago, IL 60611. All require the Medical College Admissions Test and most a bachelor's degree. A four-year curriculum includes a final year of supervised practice. Licensure by states on examination; usually reciprocal from state to state.

Pharmacy: A five-year undergraduate program. Schools are accredited by the American Council on Pharmaceutical Education, Inc., 1 E. Wacker Dr., Chicago, IL 60601. Information also from The American Pharmaceutical Association, 2215 Constitution Ave., NW, Washington, DC 20037. Graduates with one year of experience are eligible for state licensure by examination. Reciprocity usual for experienced practitioners.

Public Health: Graduate programs accredited by the American Public Health Association, Inc., 1015 18th St., NW, Washington, DC 20036.

Speech Pathology and Audiology: Graduate programs accredited by the American Speech and Hearing Association, 9030 Old Georgetown Rd., Washington, DC 20014. Certification of practitioner by same. Teaching certificate also needed to work in public schools in some states.

Veterinary Medicine: Four years beyond entry after minimum of two years of college. State licensure; not always reciprocal. Accrediting agency is the American Veterinary Medical Association, 930 North Meacham Rd., Schaumburg, IL 60172.

Education:

All states certify the qualifications of public school teachers, administrators, guidance workers and frequently school librarians, through their departments of education. College programs of teacher preparation are accredited by the National Council for Accreditation of Teacher Education, 1750 Pennsylvania Ave., NW, Washington, DC 20006.

State certification requirements vary a great deal and periodic summaries are published by the National Education Association of the U.S., 1201 Sixteenth St., NW, Washington, DC 20036 and titled *A Manual on Certification Requirements for School Personnel in the United States*. Within particular states, interested students should seek the counsel of their individual state departments of education. General information is available from the U.S. Department of Health, Education and Welfare, Washington, DC 20202 and the National Education Association (see above).

Engineering:

College programs are accredited by the Engineers' Council for Professional Development, 345 East 47th St., New York, NY 10017. In all states, engineers whose work may affect life, health, or property, must be licensed or registered. Registration usually involves graduation from an accredited school and some specific amount and/or type of experience. General information may be obtained from the American Society for Engineering Education, One Dupont Circle, NW, Washington, DC 20036.

Several other occupational fields and the preparatory education for entering them are influenced to some extent by various accrediting agencies:

Architecture: National Architectural Accrediting Board, 1735 New York Ave. NW, Washington, DC 20006. See also the Association of Collegiate Schools of Architecture, same address, and the American Institute of Architects, 1735 New York Ave., NW, Washington, DC 20006.

Art: National Association of Schools of Art, 11250 Roger Bacon Dr., Reston, VA 20090.

Business: American Assembly of Collegiate Schools of Business, Office Parkway, St. Louis, MO 63130. Many approved graduate schools require the Admissions Test for Graduate Study in Business.

Chemistry: American Chemical Society, 1155 16th St., NW, Washington, DC 20036. Graduates of accredited undergraduate programs are eligible for membership in this organization after certain experience.

Forestry: Society of American Foresters, Gifford Pinchot Forestry Bldg., Wild Acres, 5400 Grosvenor Lane, Bethesda, MD 20014.

Journalism and Communications: American Council on Education for Journalism, University of Missouri, Columbia, MO 65201.

Landscape Architecture: American Society of Landscape Architects, 1750 Old Meadow Rd., McLean, VA 22101.

Librarianship: American Library Association, 50 East Huron St., Chicago, IL 60611. Basic program is a five-year master's degree.

Music: National Association of Schools of Music, 11250 Roger Bacon Dr., Reston, VA 20090.

Psychology: Only doctoral programs in clinical or counseling psychology are accredited by the American Psychological Association, 1200 17th St., NW, Washington, DC 20036.

Social Work: Both undergraduate (baccalaureate) and graduate programs are accredited by the Council on Social Work Education, 345 East 46th St., New York, NY 10017. Individual certification and professional membership is by and in the National Association of Social Workers, 1425 H St., NW, Washington, DC 20005. Also refer to: American Sociological Association, 1722 N St., NW, Washington, DC 20036. For full NASW membership, a practitioner must be graduated from a CSWE accredited program.

Theology: Association of Theological Schools in the United States and Canada. Mostly accreditation of Protestant schools and seminaries. Address is: P.O. Box 396, Vandalia, OH 45377.

Obviously, all persons considering undergraduate transfer to a program (such as librarianship, nursing, optometry, occupational or physical therapy, social work and the like) or admission to a graduate program in law, medicine, osteopathy, clinical or counseling psychology, etc., should be sure the program has appropriate accreditation. Information may be found in *American Universities and Colleges* published by the American Council on Education, One Dupont Circle, NW, Washington, DC 20036, as well as from the organizations previously listed.

In some of the fields mentioned, selective control of admissions by colleges amounts to restriction of the number and qualification of the practitioners of the profession. For some time the medical professions especially have been sharply criticized for restrictive practices. Nonetheless, the process of gaining admission to a medical school is highly competitive at any time and will likely remain so for a long time. When jobs for baccalaureate graduates are scarce, applications for graduate schools increase thus aggravating the competitive factor. Recently, competition has been strong in law, social work, clinical psychology and some other fields. Despite the pressure of competition and the requirements by some schools for nationally administered examinations, graduate schools do vary considerably in their emphasis on specific admissions criteria. Each student should begin the assessment of further opportunities early and get all the pertinent information from as many schools as may be feasible.

In addition to the specific professional accreditation requirements mentioned, the following occupations are restricted or regulated by some or all states: appliance repair technicians, automotive mechanics, barbers, chiropractors, cosmetologists, electricians, embalmers and funeral directors, engineers and land surveyors, hairdressers, hospital administrators, nursing home administrators, plumbers, podiatrists, psychologists, public accountants, radio and TV technicians, real estate brokers, and sanitarians. This list is not exhaustive.

In other academic fields, while there may be no formal accreditation, there are professional associations to which most recognized scholars in the field belong. Early and active membership is thus almost a requirement for professional status. The names of these organizations run the alphabetical gamut from the Aaron Burr Association to the Young Printing Executives Club. To list them all would fill several hundred pages.* Each student should inquire from an academic counselor the names of the appropriate organization in his or her field of career interest.

The student will also gain increased awareness by surveying the range of graduate programs now offered by major universities and by simply inquiring of the professionals with whom he/she comes into contact. Almost all fields are becoming more complex and double, triple, multi-specialties are proliferating. A librarian must now have some background in computer usage, techniques of replication, and in many instances a multiplicity of vocabularies to encompass one or several technical fields.

These new multi-disciplinary specialties are created first as an individual response to a need. If the response is successful, it leads to proliferation of the specialty and eventually to some formalization of educational and experience requirements. Such specialties are arising at the interface of the aerospace and ecological sciences and in advanced areas of all sciences, especially the behavioral and informational.

Also emerging in several fields is the team approach in which a number of persons of different disciplines and levels of responsibility work together on a problem.

Some occupations, being related to basic human needs are found virtually everywhere. Basic medical and allied health service occupations, education, merchandising and distribution, law protective occupations and such exist wherever people live. Because they relate to people, more jobs in these occupations exist in compacted urban areas.

Some occupations are limited to one or a few geographical areas. Examples would be mining, automobile production, aerospace, electronics research and design, large scale commercial agriculture, public relations, motion picture production and many others. These occupations are geographically concentrated because of their dependence on natural resources, the availability of specific modes of distribution, or simply historical development (such as the Wall Street home for stock market trading).

Centralization leads to centralization as talent tends to accumulate in one area. This is the nature of certain occupational fields and our magalopolitical society.

---

* A second edition of *Career Guide to Professional Associations: A Directory of Organizations by Occupational Field* was published in 1980 by The Carroll Press, Cranston, R.I. 02920.

Section III: TECHNIQUES FOR CAREER IMPLEMENTATION

Chapter Five

THE CAREER DEVELOPMENT PROCESS: AN OVERVIEW

by

Thomas J. McEneaney

As the number of students in colleges and universities increased during the last twenty-five years, the professionals employed in the offices designed to provide services to these students have changed their attitudes and their techniques appreciably.

Formerly offices designed to assist students with the formulation and advancement of their career plans were known by such names as Appointment Bureaus, Placement Bureaus, Placement Offices. Today we find increasing emphasis on the counseling functions that always were a significant aspect of the work accomplished in these offices. Consistent with the change in emphasis we find more and more of these offices incorporating such words as development, planning, life, counseling and careers into their designated titles. In our own case, we have recently changed our title from the Office of Graduate Placement Services to the Career Development and Placement Office.

The size and scope of these offices will vary from campus to campus. They will include some or all of the following functions: testing, counseling, part-time employment, summer employment, college recruiting, business, industrial, governmental, educational and alumni activities, and financial aid. In some cases, some of these activities will be assigned to other departments within the college or university, or these services may not be offered at all. The effectiveness with which the office operates will be in a direct proportion to the primacy of the operation as viewed by the chief administrator, since adequate facilities, staff, student loads, etc., require expenditure of monies and are thus economic in nature.

To a larger degree, the activities of the offices we are speaking about, irrespective of their nomenclature, subscribe and embody the following "Philosophy of College Placement" adopted by the College Placement Council, Inc.

The Philosophy of
Career Planning and Placement

The goal of the educative process is the development of the individual in order that potential both as an individual and as a constructive member of society may be fulfilled.

The focus of Career Planning and Placement Services is upon the student not only immediately before and after graduation, but also during the earlier undergraduate years in the quest for self-understanding, appraisal of interests and abilities, and efforts to determine vocational objectives which are most meaningful and satisfying.

55

It is the purpose of career counseling and placement referral to assist students and graduates in these endeavors, functioning as an integral part of the educative process.

Career Planning and Placement has the responsibility to develop and maintain communication channels among students, faculty, educational administrators, educational institutions, and employers so that their various needs and interests can be properly interpreted and implemented.

(Career Planning and Placement is used to designate the name of the service; career counseling and placement referral to designate functions performed within the service.)

(Adopted by the College Placement Council Inc., January, 1972)

In our own case here at Northeastern, we have divided our Career Development and Placement Office into two major divisions as follows: (a) Business and Technical Placement and (b) Social Science and Allied Health Placement. The professional staff in the former are responsible for undergraduate and graduate students in the science areas of the Colleges of Arts and Science, Business Administration, Engineering, University and Lincoln Colleges (part-time degree programs of a technical and non-technical nature) and the College of Criminal Justice and alumni of these colleges. This division of the department also administers the campus recruiting program. We will have more to say with regard to this program later in this chapter. Professional specialists with backgrounds in business, criminal justice and engineering are provided to service the needs of the students in this area.

In the latter group we have professionally trained counselors to service students in the humanities, social sciences, education (physical), leisure, elementary, secondary, counseling (school and community), reading, special education, administration, as well as students in Nursing, Pharmacy, Physical Therapy and Allied Health.

We also have professional personnel to handle our foreign and international students and provide counseling within this framework for students who are interested in continuing their education beyond the baccalaureate degree. The foregoing is presented here merely to provide the reader with a sample of how one particular large-urban university office happens to handle its case load from an administrative view. Other colleges and universities will have varying types of structures designed to specifically meet the needs of their student populations.

An analogy from The Fisherman's Creed may serve to reflect change that has occurred in the last quarter of a century.

"Give me a fish and I will eat today — Teach me to fish and I will eat for a lifetime." Twenty-five years ago, I think we were more devoted to bringing job openings to the attention of students and alumni. Today, I feel vocational counselors are spending increasing amounts of time and effort in a truly pedagogical effort designed to provide greater self understanding, appraisal of interests and abilities, determination of vocational goals that are meaningful and satisfying with appropriate emphasis on the value of communication skills and the components of the decision-making process. Other facets of the changing process are that greater efforts are being made to work with students *throughout* their college careers and that a goodly portion of things that were formerly done on an individual counseling basis are now done in groups with individual counseling sessions being more personal-problem oriented.

Other evidence of our changing environment is that formerly there was more emphasis placed on a life-time career with one or two employers whereas today we recognize a number of vocational changes as being an integral part of a vocational career pattern.

As we enter the decade of the eighties, the Occupational Outlook for college graduates indicates "that the number of labor force entrants having a college degree is expected to continue to exceed openings in the types of jobs traditionally sought by graduates. About three graduates out of four are expected to continue to find the kinds of jobs sought by graduates, but about one graduate in four will have to enter non-traditional occupations or face unemployment. Like graduates in the early and mid-seventies, future graduates may have to work harder at finding jobs and may be less likely to find jobs in the occupation of their choice than were graduates during the 1960's."

"Greater efforts in energy production, transportation, and environmental protection will contribute to a growing demand for scientists, engineers and technicians. The medical professions can be expected to grow as the health services industry expands. The demand for professional workers to develop and utilize computer resources is also projected to grow rapidly."

All of the above indicates that college students will have to have effective training in job search strategies. An encapsulated version of this process follows.

The College Student: Job Search Strategies

Just as most practical people consult and plan with organizations such as travel agencies, the American Automobile Association, etc. when planning travel to places they are unfamiliar with, so should college students place a *priority* on visiting these college placement bureaus to determine the amount and degree of assistance they may obtain in charting a course with which they are, at best, casually familiar.

Much to your surprise you will probably find that a wealth of material is available to you, from general brochures on the components of job search strategies to definitive information on many areas of vocational endeavors in which you have an interest.

The obvious starting place seems to be to determine what makes you, as a complex psychological organism tick — how the sum total of your life experiences have impacted on your personal growth and development. This examination is going to embrace physical and mental characteristics, personality traits, ambitions and interests, as well as abilities and aptitude. The foregoing types of information constitute what is referred to professionally as "self-analysis." It represents the meaningful critical point in effective vocational planning and is something that can be accomplished only by the individual. Subsequent counseling and testing are mere adjuncts to meaningful self-analysis.

Mrs. Cornelia Ladwig, a colleague at West Virginia University, approaches this topic somewhat differently, referring to a "skill-bank." Her approach follows:

> In a sense, the graduate has already experienced everything he will ever do. He has demonstrated ability to analyze, plan and organize, to lead, communicate, listen, persuade, create, combine ideas with manipulative skills, work under pressure of deadlines, reason numerically, develop goals and apply sustained efforts to accomplish them, identify ethical and moral issues which impinge on methodology and decision, serve others, and to search out and draw upon appropriate sources of information. These functions form his skill-bank.
>
> He has done these things in his academic life, in his hobbies, in his part-time jobs, in his volunteer community and church activities. Because of proficiency in one or more of these areas he may even have been attracted to some career, perhaps without fully realizing the reason why. Since each job emphasizes certain of these skills more than others, the first step in his preparation will be to examine his skill-bank to determine whether he has the necessary skill in his account. He will probably find it necessary to become thoroughly acquainted with each of the items in his skill-bank. For example, he will note the kinds of situations in which he has been an efficient leader, and perhaps the dimensions of particular incidents in which he functioned less effectively. He will begin to see that the kinds of people involved, the kinds of tasks involved, and the pressures involved, are all related in determining the degree of success he has had as a leader. Such analysis also identifies the type of situations in which he was more likely to wait for suggestions from others than to initiate action.
>
> He should examine the remaining skills in his account in the same manner, so that he is not only able to identify the areas in which he has proficiency, but also to locate the combinations of these skills which are most effective.[2]

After you have completed the introspective study, the next step is to determine where you will market the talents that you have determined you possess. This facet of your market survey is called "occupational analysis." The objective is to decide on an industry and a position within this industry which will fulfill your psychological needs and provide you with a satisfying and rewarding employment situation. In the event that you are unable to reduce this data to a specific position title, you must be able to communicate with a description of the types of skills you possess that will make you a potentially valuable employee of this organization. In using this approach, the interviewer should be provided with sufficient information which he or she may interpret and relate to specific positions within the organization.

The third step in the procedure is to create a meaningful advertisement of your abilities. Specific items of personal information about your educational, vocational and military background (if applicable) should be brought together in an attractive and concise document called by many different names in the profession viz. resume, qualification record, personal data sheet, to name a few. Since this topic is covered in greater detail elsewhere in this text, it is not necessary to elaborate here.

There is only one remaining step in the process. This is the crucial step of selling yourself to potential employers through the medium of the interview. This may be done in any of the following ways: direct contact with an employer; college recruiting programs; or indirect contact with an employer utilizing friends, acquaintances or a commercial employment agency as an intermediary. Further information in Chapter 8.

It is in this area that the adequacy of your verbal and written communicative skills will serve either materially to assist or defeat your vocational objectives. College seniors who have weaknesses in either of these areas should utilize their senior year to maximize these abilities.

The College Recruiting Process:

In the remaining portion of this chapter, we will limit our discussion to college recruiting programs. Although this represents the focal point around which the discussion is oriented, most of the content may be broadly applied to any step in the employment process.

College recruiting and college relations is an area of personnel activity which has developed considerable momentum since the conclusion of hostilities in World War II. Basically, it is a medium through which national organizations (business, industrial and governmental) visit the nation's campuses to evaluate collegiate talent as related to their individual employment needs. Successful campus recruitment is a highly competitive process, as is the attainment of any professional level position. Roughly twenty applicants will be interviewed for each position that is awarded.

In many instances vocational aspirations may have to be temporarily adjusted in accordance with the number and types of positions available in a particular job family. Certainly, it is imperative that applicants possess the greatest amount of flexibility with respect to geographic locations, types of positions that they will consider, etc. The limitations an individual imposes both on the locale and type of work acceptable to him will accomplish nothing more than increase his chance of a more lengthy period of unemployment. The period will tend to increase according to a geometric progression as opposed to an arithmetic one.

The process commences with an organization establishing interviewing dates on the college campuses that it wishes to visit. This determination is often predicated on departmental strengths in a particular institution, as well as on the relative availability of talent in a particular discipline nationally. The scheduling of dates is usually accomplished a minimum of one year in advance, with placement offices deciding the final dates for interviewing on campus.

As the recruiting season approaches, the placement office posts the requirements and specifications of the participating organizations. At the same time, students who are both interested and qualified are encouraged to sign up for interview appointments. Students should review employer files to ascertain if the organization appears to have the types of employment opportunities they are seeking in geographic locations that are acceptable. If so, they establish a mutually convenient appointment time, and subsequently appear at the appointed time and place for their interview.

The campus interview, the initial step in the employment process, is referred to as a "preliminary" or "screening" interview due to its brevity. During the twenty or thirty minute period consumed by this interview, candidates are either placed in a "further action" classification or are rejected. Candidates who are rejected usually do not meet the requirements of the potential employing organization or have manifested some undesirable personality factor.

The qualifications of candidates who pass the initial screening interview at a specific school are then placed in a pool with the qualifications of other candidates who passed their screening interviews at other schools visited by the organization.

Additional criteria are then applied to the applications remaining by departmental managers. It is the managers having vacancies to whom the applications are circulated. In this process a percentage of the applications are eliminated; the remaining applicants are then invited to visit one of the facilities of the potential employer. During this visit which traditionally consumes one-half to a full day (in certain cases, two days may be required), the applicant is subjected to one or more interviews in greater depth and, not infrequently, to a series of pre-employment tests as well.

Usually the applicant is provided luncheon as a guest of the organization. Quite frequently the organization will provide a host who is roughly the same age as the applicant and has been hired within the last three years. The potential employee can candidly discuss pertinent matters and problems that may enable him to more accurately evaluate the desirability of this organization as the place in which he wishes to launch his vocational career. This should be a friendly, anything-goes (assuming acceptable limits) type of luncheon.

At the conclusion of this phase of the process, if he is successful, the applicant will receive a formal offer of employment.

Earlier we stated a requisite skill in the enterprise of effective vocational planning was good communicative skills, both oral and written. The applicant should be particularly aware of how he or she sounds in verbal interactions during the interviewing process. This situation is probably best exemplified by an experience that took place some years ago. A student of mine whose scholastic attainment was excellent had a speech problem which was the result of both environmental factors and socio-economic background. Knowing that his speech patterns would be a limiting factor in the business to which he aspired, I scheduled an appointment with him to discuss casually some of the areas we were covering in our class discussions. Prior to seeing him, I turned on my tape recorder and recorded the ensuing discussion. After approximately twenty minutes I inquired as to whether he had ever had an opportunity to listen to himself speak. He replied negatively and I then explained that I had been recording our conversation and wished to replay it. As the recording was replayed, he was obviously amazed. "My God, is that me?" he remarked. With this little insight and some abbreviated counseling, he was able to make marked improvements in his diction during the remainder of the year.

Written communication is an integral part of any job campaign as well. You will undoubtedly find yourself either directing unsolicited communications to organizations without possible available opportunities or writing letters in reply to advertisements. Letters of appreciation for interviews you have had are an excellent way of keeping one's application active. Finally, letters requesting extensions of time for considering job offers, letters of rejection, and letters of acceptance are all part of the written communications involved in a job campaign.

Keep in mind particularly in relation to job offers that any communication becomes part of your employee file. Spelling errors, poor word choice and awkward structure may haunt you for the first several years of employment since your file will be reviewed in detail whenever you are subject to review, promotion, etc. If you have weaknesses in this area, be careful before you post the acceptance letter that your employer's reaction upon receiving it is not to question his own judgment in having extended the offer of employment to you. In the words of Edward Fitzgerald:

> *The Moving Finger writes; and having writ,*
> *Moves on; nor all your Piety nor Wit*
> *Shall have it back to cancel half a line*
> *Nor all your Tears wash out a Word of it.*[3]

Earlier in this chapter we spoke about the fact that organizations invite potential employees to visit them, at their expense. Reimbursement, needless to say, covers only the actual expenses of the recruiting trip and should not include entertainment or personal expenditures.

Reimbursement policies vary. Some return the applicant's funds the same day, while others take from two to four weeks to complete reimbursement proceedings. Thus, it is necessary for college seniors to have funds at hand for recruiting expenses.

Receipts

Hotel and travel receipts will normally be required before reimbursement can be made.

Travel

You may select the most convenient means of public transportation, either tourist-class air or first-class rail. In your travel expense report, indicate the complete route for which your tickets were purchased. If you make your trip by automobile, show your complete route and mileage. Report any intermediate stopover points.

Includes airport limousine service, local or suburban trains, and taxis.

Meals

This item should cover meals, tax and tips and should be listed on a daily basis.

Receipts should be obtained. Applicants are cautioned to be prudent (not stingy) in this area.

Baggage

Baggage service tips normally cover transfer of baggage at the airport, hotel or other travel center. Checking service charges may be included.

General Information

Be prudent! Remember that all major companies have learned the normal costs of travel expenses through daily experience. If an angry company comptroller returns your expense account it usually means that his firm has terminated its consideration of you as an applicant, irrespective of your skills.

The following items are NOT considered normal business expenses:

1. Entertainment, tours, cigarettes, magazines, etc.

2. Insurance, interest on loans, excessive tips (should not exceed 20 percent of the food bill).

3. Personal phone calls, except in emergencies or for recruitment business.

4. Hotel stopovers at points other than the city being visited, except as may be required by the transportation schedule.

5. Valet expenses, except under special circumstances, e.g., when a one-day interview schedule was originally arranged and the company asks the student to stay an additional day or two.

6. Expenses for persons other than the individual invited on a plant visit, except where the company authorizes expenses for the applicant's spouse.

When you visit more than one firm on the same recruiting trip, you will be expected to pro-rate your expenses among all of them. In the event that you are traveling by a commercial carrier, the first step in this process is to duplicate the ticket by a photo-copying process. The number of copies needed is one more than the total number of firms to be visited on the trip. The additional copy is for your own personal records. Since this procedure seems to create the greatest number of problems, several examples follow which, hopefully, will clarify the situation.

Illustration 1 assumes Mr. Allen is visiting the Myopia Corporation in Washington, D.C. and has been advised to arrive the evening before the interview date.

Illustration 2 assumes that Mr. Allen is visiting the Standard Oil Company, Cleveland, Ohio and the Joslyn Manufacturing and Supply Company in Chicago, Illinois on a single trip. In both cases, the organizations suggested arrival on the evening before the interview date.

Illustration 3, Mr. Allen has waited until the interview program was almost over before making plant visits. To conserve time, he visits the Campbell Soup Company, Unity Corporation and Joslyn Manufacturing and Supply Company on a consolidated trip to the Chicago area.

All illustrations assume luncheon tabs are picked up by the host company.

After receiving a formal offer of employment, the candidate should acknowledge its receipt (Illustration D) and provide the employer with an indication of the time when he will act on the offer. Needless to say, it is imperative that he take this action within the time period specified,

Due to the fact that this revision is being prepared during a period of widely fluctuating prices, actual costs have been eliminated from these illustrations. Conceptually, how the costs should be prorated is indicated with the belief that the student can successfully handle the allocation of costs according to the formula.

ILLUSTRATION 1

Trip to a single firm in Washington, D.C. from Boston, Massachusetts requiring overnight hotel accommodations.

> Limousine to Logan International Airport
> Air Fare (Boston, Mass. to Washington, D.C. and return (tourist)
> Dinner (night before visit)
> Breakfast (day of visit)
> Lunch (guest of organization)
> Dinner (day of visit)*
> Taxi to Statler Hilton from National Airport
> Taxi from Statler Hilton to Myopia Corporation
> Taxi from Myopia Corporation to National Airport
> Statler Hilton Hotel Bill
> Gratuities
> Limousine from Logan International Airport-Boston
>
> *Only applicable on date of visit if return is later than 6:30 P.M.
>
> All expenses are charged to the Myopia Corporation

ILLUSTRATION 2

Single trip in which more than one visitation is made.

Limousine to Logan International Airport	(1)
Air Fare (tourist class) – Boston, MA. – Cleveland, Ohio	(1)
Limousine to Statler Hilton from Hopkins Airport	(1)
Gratuity	(1)
Statler Hilton Hotel Bill	(1)
Dinner (night before visit)	(1)
Breakfast (day of visit)	(1)
Taxi to Standard Oil of Ohio (1)	(1)
Luncheon (day of visit - organization guest)	
Taxi from Standard Oil to Hopkins Airport	(1)
Air Fare (tourist class) to Chicago (O'Hare Field)	(2)
Limousine from O'Hare Field to Conrad Hilton	(2)
Conrad Hilton Hotel Bill	(2)
Dinner (night before visit)	(2)
Breakfast (day of visit)	(2)
Gratuities	(2)
Taxi to Joslyn Manufacturing & Supply Company (2)	(2)
Taxi from Joslyn Co. to O'Hare Airport	(2)
Dinner (day of visit)	(2)
Air Fare (tourist class) O'Hare Field to Logan Airport	(2)
Limousine from Logan International Airport to Boston	(2)

Standard Oil of Ohio (1)   Total expenses assigned to Company 1
Joslyn Manufacturing & Supply Co. (2)   Total expenses assigned to Company 2
Proration of expenses between both companies = total amount of bill.

ILLUSTRATION 3

Multiple Visitation within a city

Limousine to Logan International Airport	1-2-3
Air Fare (tourist class) Boston, MA. to Chicago, Ill.	1-2-3
Limousine from O'Hare Field to Conrad Hilton	1-2-3
Dinner (night before visitation)	1
Gratuities	1-2-3
Breakfast (day of visitation)	1
Taxi to Joslyn Manufacturing & Supply Company (1)	1
Taxi from Joslyn Manufacturing & Supply Company	1
Dinner (evening of first visitation day)	2
Breakfast (2nd visitation day)	2
Taxi to Campbell Soup Company (2)	2
Taxi from Campbell Soup Company to Conrad Hilton Hotel	2
Dinner (2nd visitation day)	3
Breakfast (3rd visitation day)	3
Taxi to Unity Corporation from Conrad Hilton	3
Taxi to Conrad Hilton from Unity Corporation	3
Dinner (3rd visitation day)	3
Conrad Hilton Hotel Bill	1-2-3
Breakfast	3
Taxi to O'Hare Field from Conrad Hilton Hotel	1-2-3
Limousine from Logan International Airport	1-2-3

Joslyn Manufacturing & Supply Company (1)
Campbell Soup Company (2)
Unity Corporation (3)
Proration of expenses between all three companies equals total amount of bill.

Earlier in this chapter we indicated that if the preliminary or campus interview was successful that the next step in the process would be for the potential employer to invite the applicant to visit the employer's facilities. (See letter *Illustration A*).

Accordingly, let us assume that Messrs. Allen & Markham were invited to visit the Anitron Corporation and that both students were sufficiently interested to accept the invitation to visit this facility. Let us also assume that as a result of the plant visitation, the organization was no longer interested in Mr. Markham, but their interest in Mr. Allen was sustained.

The next step would be for the employer to indicate the status of their applications to these two men in a letter as illustrated below:

Illustration B — Sample rejection letter

Illustration C — Sample offer of employment

In *Illustration C,* the letter offering employment, no specific expiration date is expressed. Many companies indicate a date by which the offer is automatically invalidated if not accepted especially when the market is tight (more persons available than positions).

After receiving a formal offer of employment, the candidate should acknowledge its receipt *(Illustration D)* and provide the employer with an indication of the time when he will act on the offer. Needless to say, it is imperative that he take this action within the time period specified, as David does in *Illustration E.*

Illustration F represents a typical employer's reply to David's rejection of the offer.

Illustration G represents the response David might have received had he rejected Anitron's offer and accepted the offer of another employing organization.

In the event that David had been most impressed with Anitron's offer and had concluded that this was the organization with which he wished to launch his career, he would merely have accepted the offer immediately *(Illustration H)*. Finally, once he has accepted this offer, he must notify all other employers with whom he had interviewed of his decision and request them to withdraw his name from further consideration. *Illustration I* indicates a typical reply from an employer to acceptance of an offer.

Alumni Placement

Practically every college and university is equipped to offer some degree of service to its alumni. In some situations, service is limited to a specific number of years beyond graduation. This is predicated on the institution's belief that it is in a position to better serve the alumnus whose experience is limited.

An alumnus contemplating using the placement service of the institution he attended should call in advance (approximately two weeks) and establish a mutually convenient appointment. Those who merely drop in without an appointment overlook the real situation that these offices are traditionally overworked and understaffed. The alumnus ends up being frustrated because the placement counselor is unable to see him and the placement counselor tends to feel pressured by the demands upon his already overworked staff.

College placement services are comparable to those of commercial employment agencies except that the service is usually free. However, education graduates quite often will be expected to pay a nominal fee to defray the cost of preparing and processing professional credentials, which are an integral part of educational placement.

Employment agencies derive their support from fees paid either by the employers or by the individual clients seeking to relocate. Employers generally pay a specific service charge. Individuals pay a fee which represents a fixed percentage of the annual salary derived from the position obtained through the employment agency. Commercial agencies are of maximum value when few positions in the labor market are being advertised.

In dealing with an institutional placement office or a commercial agency, the applicant will usually be required to present himself for a personal interview. He will also be required to furnish a specified number of up-to-date resumes. In certain cases, the client will be expected to provide employment references or grant permission for the counselor to obtain them directly.

Once the registration process is completed, the school agency will refer positions which are registered with them to qualified applicants until such time as the applicant is satisfactorily employed. Applicants should keep in mind that the referrals sent to them constitute a form of privileged communication and should not be shared with friends. Applicants also have the responsibility of keeping the counselor advised of their status. When they have finally found a suitable position, applicants should advise their counselor of the name of the employing firm, position title, starting date and salary. This is most important when dealing with institutions and, should be accomplished even though employment may have occurred through other channels.

Commercial agencies have more refined administrative and control procedures. Their referral forms are usually designed to serve a dual purpose. First, they notify the registered applicant of a position; and second, they serve as an introductory device to the potential employer. Applicants present these forms to the employer's representative at the time of the interview. At the conclusion of the interview, the employer completes the forms and returns them to the agency with his evaluation of the applicant. He also indicates whether the candidate is to be employed or not.

Generally speaking, placement counselors employed by educational institutions will evidence a more sincere personal interest in candidates seeking their service since they are salaried employees of the institution. Most agency personnel, on the other hand, receive, at best, a very small guaranteed stipend from the agency owner. The remainder of their remuneration occurs as a percentage of the fee charged the client. Many agency representatives, therefore, tend to "sell" applicants positions rather than attempting to find the type of position the qualified applicant seeks. Usually the better agencies will hold membership in the National Employment Board and will have evidence of their membership prominently displayed.

Finally, the role of the computer in the employment process should not be overlooked. Many commercial agencies and some college placement offices are utilizing computers in the job-matching process.

In the foregoing material you have been exposed to a brief summary of the various steps involved in the selection process. Hopefully, this review will help you as you seek employment.

The following excerpts from guidelines established by the College Placement Association will help you understand the operations of a college placement office during the on-campus recruiting by employers.

PRINCIPLES and PRACTICES: College Career Planning, Placement and Recruitment

A statement of basic agreements developed for those engaged in career planning, placement and recruitment as a guide to ethical practice. This document pertains particularly to the inter-relationships and activities of college career planning and placement staffs, candidates (students and graduates) and employers. It is assumed that all those engaged in college career planning, placement and recruitment will be aware of and comply with all government regulations applying to employment.

PRINCIPLES

It is in the best interests of candidates, colleges, and employers alike that the consideration of careers and selection of employment opportunities be based on an understanding of all the relevant facts and that these considerations be made in an atmosphere conducive to objective thought.

The recruiting of college students and graduates for employment should be carried out by the employers, candidates, and college authorities to serve best the following objectives:

1. The open and free selection of employment opportunities that will provide candidates with the optimum long-term utilization of their talents, consistent with their personal objectives.

2. The promotion of intelligent and responsible choice of careers by the candidates for their own greatest satisfaction and the most fruitful long-range investment of their talents for themselves, for their employers, and for society.

3. The development of the placement function as an integral part of the educational system so that it, as well as the total recruiting process, may be oriented toward the establishment of high standards of integrity and conduct among all parties.

GUIDELINES FOR OPERATION

Employers

In direct on-campus recruiting activities, an employing organization should be represented by its own personnel. In all other recruiting activities, the employing organization is expected to assume responsibility for all representations made in its name and in accordance with the Principles and Practices of College Career Planning, Placement and Recruitment.

The presentation of career job information should be made in a knowledgeable, ethical and responsible fashion.

Ethical salary administation principles are expected to be followed.

Special payments, gifts, bonuses, or other inducements should not be offered.

All conditions of employment, including starting salaries, should be explained clearly to candidates prior to or at the time of the offer of employment.

Reasonable time to consider an offer should be given candidates. In no case should candidates be subjected to undue pressure to make a decision concerning employment.

Preferential service should not be requested of any college placement office.

Individual salary offers made by other employers should not be solicited by an employer.

Employer material should be supplied in sufficient quantities and well in advance of interviewing dates.

Candidates' visit to employers' premises should be arranged to interfere as little as possible with class schedules. Details of such visits should be carefully explained to the candidate.

Career Planning and Placement Offices

Competent career counseling and other assistance to aid candidates in reaching career decisions should be available.

Career literature and employment material should be made available to candidates and faculty members.

Candidates should be urged to file resumes and/or related placement material in the career planning and placement office. Such materials shall be maintained in accordance with the rules and regulations concerning confidentiality of records and shall be released in accordance with the directions of the candidate.

Candidates

Both written and oral material presented by a candidate should be an honest statement of relevant data.

Reimbursement for visits at an employer's expense should be only for those expenditures pertinent to the trip. If other employers are visited on the same trip, the cost should be prorated.

The employer's deadline for acceptance of offers of employment should be met unless an extension has been obtained from the employer.

If candidates have legitimate reasons for the extended consideration of more than one offer, they should not only notify employers whose offers they are refusing, but also communicate with employers under consideration to attempt to establish mutually satisfactory decision dates. They should make their final choice at the earliest practicable date.

Acceptance of an employment offer should be made in good faith and with sincere intention to honor the commitment.

In preparation for interviews with prospective employers, candidates should analyze their interests and abilities, consider their career objectives, seek information about the fields of their interest through published materials and counseling, and organize their thoughts so that they may ask and answer questions intelligently.

Before an interview, candidates should read the employer's materials and fill out such forms as may be required. The candidate should observe recommended procedures as to interviews.

Interview appointments should be arranged as early as practicable and in accordance with the career planning and placement office's procedures. Necessary cancellations should be made in keeping with that office's procedures.

An invitation to visit an employer's premises should be acknowledged promptly and should be accepted only when there is a sincere interest in a position with that employer. Arrangements should be made sufficiently in advance to permit mutual confirmation of dates.

Decisions concerning employment and terms of employment where practicable should be communicated to the career planning and placement office.

FOOTNOTES

1.   "The Philosophy of Career Planning and Placement." Bethlehem, Pa., The College Placement Council, 1972. Reprinted by permission.

2.   Ladwig, Cornelia, "Before the Interview," *The College Placement Annual,* 1967, p. 15.

3.   Fitzgerald, Edward, translation of *The Rubaiyat* of Omar Khayyam, as quoted by R.J. Morrissey in "Know Whereof You Write," *The College Placement Annual,* 1961, p. 37.

Refer also to the following issues of *The College Placement Annual,* published by The College Placement Council: 1960, 1962, 1963, 1964, 1965, 1966, 1968, 1969, 1970, 1971, 1972, 1973, 1974, 1975, 1976, 1977, 1978, and 1979.

(Illustration A — Employer's invitation to visit)

ANITRON CORPORATION
Two Park Plaza
New York, New York 10010

February 11, 1981

Mr. David Allen
28 Carson Avenue
Braintree, Massachusetts 02184

Dear David:

It was a pleasure talking with you at the University and I appreciate your taking the time for an interview.

You made a very favorable impression on me. Your enthusiasm about starting your career and the interest you appear to have in the engineering aspects of systems analysis were especially noticeable.

While we cannot be sure that we will have a suitable position for you, we think it would be a good investment for both of us if you could find a convenient time to visit our office and explore the possibility further. Any day would be suitable. You will have an opportunity to learn much more about us than I was able to relate in the short conference we had. We will also have the opportunity to become better acquainted with you.

We will rely on your judgment on the selection of a date that will not interfere with your class schedule. Please call me collect; it will be easier to set a mutually convenient date.

It would be helpful if you would complete and return the enclosed application. It will provide us with information that is valuable and not always included in a personal resume. Would you also forward a recent transcript of your grades. If there is a charge, we will reimburse you.

We look forward to hearing from you soon and hope that you can find time to pay us a visit.

Very truly yours,

C. V. Alstead
Personnel Manager

CVA:mac

(Illustration B — Employer's rejection of applicant)

ANITRON CORPORATION
Two Park Plaza
New York, New York 10010

March 25, 1981

Mr. Richard Markham
14 Pineview Terrace
Waltham, Massachusetts 02154

Dear Mr. Markham:

Thank you for visiting us to discuss employment with Anitron Corporation. Those of us who met you trust we were able to give you a clear picture of the scope of activities at Anitron.

We have carefully considered your comments and desires as expressed during the interview. It is our belief that while you have a very impressive background we do not feel that we could offer the type of position which would enable you to utilize your education and training in a mutually advantageous manner.

You created a favorable impression on us. We feel that it will be only a matter of time before you find the position you desire and that you will be a definite asset to the organization you do join.

I sincerely appreciate your expressed interest in Anitron Corporation and want to take this opportunity to wish you every success in your career.

Very truly yours,

C. V. Alstead
Personnel Manager

CVA:mac

(Illustration C — Employer's offer of employment)

ANITRON CORPORATION
Two Park Plaza
New York, New York 10010

March 25, 1981

Mr. David Allen
28 Carson Avenue
Braintree, Massachusetts 02184

Dear Mr. Allen:

We enjoyed your recent visit to our facilities and trust that your discussions with our staff were informative. The people with whom you met were impressed with your qualifications and feel that you would be a definite asset to our organization.

On the basis of these discussions and your representation to us concerning your qualifications and previous experience, we are pleased to offer you a position with our Systems Analysis Department.

Your starting salary for this position will be $1670.00 per month with future professional and financial growth dependent upon your individual performance and contributions.

This offer to join Anitron is, of course, conditional until you have satisfactorily met our established employment requirements which include the execution of a patent agreement, the successful completion of our medical examination and personal history review.

If you decide to accept this offer we would appreciate your completing and returning the enclosed Employment Questionnaire immediately. You will be reimbursed in accordance with our policy for expenses incurred as a result of your move to the New York City area. We will pay travel expenses for you (and your spouse) to look over available housing at your new location. This will include motel, meals, gas and mileage for a period of up to one week. Payment will also be made for moving your household goods. You will be reimbursed for all of these expenses after you have joined the organization. Also enclosed is additional information about company policies and benefits that become available to you when you join Anitron.

We were happy to talk with you about our work here and are looking forward to your joining our organization. Your early reply regarding a decision and an indication of your proposed starting date should you accept this offer will be appreciated. If you have any questions, please feel free to call me.

Very truly yours,

C. V. Alstead
Personnel Manager

CVA:mac
Enclosures

(Illustration D — Applicant's acknowledgment of employer's offer)

28 Carson Avenue
Braintree, Mass. 02184
March 27, 1981

Mr. C. V. Alstead,
Personnel Manager
Anitron Corporation
Two Park Plaza
New York, N.Y. 10010

Dear Mr. Alstead:

This letter is to thank you for and acknowledge your offer of employment dated March 25, 1981. This communication invited me to join your Systems Analysis Department at a monthly salary of $1670.00.

While your offer of employment is most attractive, I feel that it would be to our mutual advantage to delay action with respect to this opportunity until May 1, 1981. This will provide me with ample time to evaluate the opportunities available to me as a result of our campus recruiting program.

Sincerely,

David Allen

(Illustration E — Applicant's rejection of offer in order to continue education)

28 Carson Avenue
Braintree, Mass. 02184
April 25, 1981

Mr. C. V. Alstead,
Personnel Manager
Anitron Corporation
Two Park Plaza
New York, N.Y. 10010

Dear Mr. Alstead:

On March 27th, I indicated that I would advise you as to whether or not I would be joining your Systems Analysis Department.

You may recall that in addition to exploring potential employment opportunities following my graduation, I also indicated that I was seriously considering furthering my education.

Regretfully, I must advise you that I have elected to pursue graduate studies in Business Administration and will be entering the Wharton School next September. Upon completion of this program, I would appreciate the opportunity of reinvestigating employment possibilities in your organization.

Your previous favorable action on my employment application is most appreciated.

Sincerely,

David Allen

(Illustration F — Employer's reply to rejection based on plans for continued education)

ANITRON CORPORATION
Two Park Plaza
New York, New York 10010

April 29, 1981

Mr. David Allen
28 Carson Avenue
Braintree, MA 02184

Dear Mr. Allen:

Thank you for your recent letter advising us that you have decided to continue your education. May I compliment you on your decision and wish you every success in your studies.

We look forward to meeting with you again as you approach the completion of your academic training to consider you for positions which may be available at that time.

Anitron continually strives to improve its recruiting program. We would appreciate your assisting us in appraising our existing recruiting efforts by completing the enclosed questionnaire. Please do not hesitate to be frank and critical in your response.

Your cooperation and interest in our company are greatly appreciated.

Sincerely,

C. V. Alstead
Personnel Manager

CVA:mac
Enclosure

(Illustration G — Employer's reply to rejection based on plans to accept another offer)

ANITRON CORPORATION
Two Park Plaza
New York, New York 10010

May 15, 1981

Mr. David Allen
28 Carson Avenue
Braintree, MA 02184

Dear Mr. Allen:

Thank you for letting me know that you will not be coming with us.

We are, of course, sorry to lose you but we appreciate your taking the time to come down to discuss career opportunities with us and we wish you the very best of luck for the future.

It would help us in our future recruiting if we knew whether your decision was based on geographical location, kind of work, or salary consideration. Anything you might feel free to tell us in this respect would be greatly appreciated.

Sincerely,

C. V. Alstead
Personnel Manager

CVA:mac

(Illustration H – Applicant's letter of acceptance)

28 Carson Avenue
Braintree, Mass. 02184
March 27, 1981

Mr. C. V. Alstead,
Personnel Manager
Anitron Corporation
Two Park Plaza
New York, N.Y. 10010

Dear Mr. Alstead:

I was very pleased to receive your letter of March 25, 1981 in which you invited me to become a member of your organization following graduation. I am enthusiastically accepting your offer of employment at a monthly salary of $1670.00.

The description of the duties which will be assigned to me in your Systems Analysis Department are both interesting and challenging. I am certain that my educational background and previous cooperative work experience will be of value to me and will permit me to be a contributing member of the Anitron Corporation.

I look forward to a lengthy and profitable career with Anitron and will report to your office at 8:30 A.M. on June 30, 1981.

Sincerely,

David Allen

*(Illustration I – Employer's confirmation of applicant's acceptance
and details of employment)*

ANITRON CORPORATION
**Two Park Plaza
New York, New York 10010**

April 4, 1981

Mr. David Allen
28 Carson Avenue
Braintree, Massachusetts 02184

Dear David:

Welcome to Anitron! We were pleased to receive your acceptance of our offer and sincerely believe that our association will be mutually advantageous.

Your suggested starting date of June 30, 1981 is satisfactory.

In connection with your employment, you are advised that company regulations require that you pass our pre-employment physical examination which must be administered by our medical department. If you have any cause for concern about your ability to pass this examination and you wish to be examined by your personal physician, please do so and advise us if any condition is found which might prevent you from passing our examination.

Our housing department will now begin making contacts with various apartment house owners in hopes of securing suitable accommodations for you. If you have any questions concerning relocation in the New York City area, please let me know.

Anitron Corporation will pay travel expenses for you (and your spouse) to look over available housing at your new location. This will include motel, meals, gas and mileage for a period of up to one week. Payment will also be made for moving your household goods. You will be reimbursed for all of these expenses after you have joined our organization.

For your information and interest, we are sending, under separate cover, some material furnished by the New York City Chamber of Commerce which will provide insight into the educational facilities and cultural activities in our area.

We look forward to having you with us.

Sincerely,

C. V. Alstead
Personnel Manager

CVA:mac

Chapter Six

THE EMPLOYMENT MARKET AND YOU

by

Sidney F. Austin

The *Dictionary of Occupational Titles*, published by the Bureau of Employment Security, U.S. Department of Labor, lists approximately 20,000 different job titles in 600 major classifications. The *Standard Classification Manual*, published by the U. S. Bureau of the Budget, lists thousands of different types of employers.

Somewhere in this complexity of thousands of distinct types of jobs with thousands of employers is the right combination for you: the right job with the right employer that will give you your start on a long and successful career.

There is plenty of work to be done in this world and there are not enough people to do it, so you should have no difficulty finding a job. The proper career approach, however, calls for you to look for *the* job, not *a* job. During your normal working span of about 40 years, you will probably spend as much time on your job as you will with your family, perhaps more. Where you live, how you live, your friends, and your whole standard of living will be, to a great extent, dependent on your work.

Arriving at a decision as to how and where you are to start your career takes some investment of time and effort, but it is not particularly difficult. You have already made some of the necessary decisions when you decided to go to college and when you decided on a course of study. These choices have been further refined by your exposure to various courses, working experiences, and extra-curricular activities. Basic career development has been established. This does not infer that, because of these decisions, you are now committed and must continue in the direction you have established. Many happy and successful careerists have made complete changes in objective based on exposure to new experiences, but such changes can prove costly in time and money. Intelligent choices of career alternatives made early pay off in success.

Have you decided on the direction of your career? Earlier chapters of this book have treated this subject in great detail. Now your task is to locate the employer who will provide you with the opportunity to go in this direction; an employer who needs an employee with your qualifications and willing to hire you because you have something to offer him. You may be lucky and find such an employer without much effort, but how can you be sure you are making the right decision unless you have made a thorough investigation of the alternatives? If you were in the market for a new car, it would be fool-hardy to walk into the first dealership on the street and buy the first automobile that you saw.

Considering the investment that you were about to make, you would study the various makes and models and visit several dealers to get the best price before you decided on which car to buy. To arrive at an intelligent decision concerning something that is infinitely more important, your career, it makes sense to spend a commensurate amount of time gathering appropriate information about prospective employers.

Start a Prospect File

A meaningful job campaign has to be organized, or inevitable confusion will result. Organization calls for a systematic way of recording and filing information you gather on prospective employers. Index cards are ideal for this purpose. As you gather pertinent information on job prospects and on companies you are interested in, record it on the cards, one company or job prospect to a card. Enter the name, address, and phone number of the company on the face of the card, and add any other information that you feel would be useful such as the nature of the company's product or service, names and titles of principal officers, the person you should contact, locations of branches, and number of employees. An entry as to why you are interested in this particular prospect would be particularly appropriate. The back of the card may be used to write notes on correspondence, phone calls, interviews, and follow-ups. Keep your prospect file up to date as your job campaign progresses and you will find it to be an invaluable tool.

Directories as Research Sources

A few hours of work are necessary to gather the information you need for your prospect file. Sources, mostly in the form of directories, are so numerous that it would not be possible to list them all. Those listed here are the most commonly used but are only representative of what is available. If you do not find what you need in your college placement office, check your college library or your local library. Large city libraries might even have a separate branch, such as the Kirstein Business Branch of the Boston Public Library, which will contain most of the references you need to conduct a complete survey of your chosen field.

Basic Directories

Start with a basic directory which will tell you where to look further. Such a book is *Sources of Business Information* by Edwin T. Coman, Jr. (University of California Press, Berkeley and Los Angeles, Calif.). In a number of broad areas of business activity, Coman lists trade and professional directories and publications, names and addresses of associations, and books and magazines with articles of interest to the specific field. This book is particularly valuable because it tells you how to organize your search through a bewildering array of available material to locate the information you are seeking.

Another basic directory that might be consulted is the *Guide to Listings of Manufacturers* (United States Chamber of Commerce, Washington, D.C.). This guide contains listings of the usual commercial directories, directories dealing with specific industries, and annual directories that are published by periodicals. It also contains suggested methods on how to locate information on specific firms.

Still another basic source is the *Encyclopedia of Business Information Sources* (Gale Research Company, Book Tower, Detroit, Michigan). This publication is a comprehensive guide to sources of information on specific topics. It lists source books, periodicals, organizations, directories, handbooks and bibliographies in 1,300 subject areas. It is arranged alphabetically by topic.

Standard Reference Sources

There are a number of general standard reference sources available which contain valuable information of a descriptive nature. Some of the more useful are noted here.

Thomas' Register of American Manufacturers (Thomas Publishing Co., 461 Eighth Avenue, New York, N.Y.). This publication, consisting of twelve volumes contains detailed information on leading manufacturing organizations throughout the country. Names and addresses of companies are listed under product headings, classified by state and city. Capital ratings of the organizations are also included. Volume 7 identifies the owners of trademarks and brand names and also lists local Chambers of Commerce and other Boards of Trade. Volumes 9-12 are a "Catalog of Companies."

MacRae's Blue Book (MacRae's Blue Book Co., 903 Burlington Avenue, Western Springs, Illinois). Consisting of four volumes, this publication lists the names and addresses of companies alphabetically, classified by product and trade name. Included in the listings are the locations of branches and the capital rating of the company.

Poor's Register of Corporation Directors and Executives (Standard and Poor Corp., 345 Hudson St., New York, N.Y.) lists thousands of leading business firms, their products, number of employees and the names and positions of their key employees.

Moody's Manual of Investment (Moody's Investors Service, Inc., 99 Church St., New York, N.Y.) provides financial information, location of principal plants, history, business and products, and the names of management personnel of companies whose stock is traded on the exchanges.

The *Million Dollar Directory* and the *Middle Market Directory* (Dun and Bradstreet, Inc., 99 Church Street, New York, N.Y.). These volumes give officers, products, approximate sales and number of employees of thousands of companies with indicated net worth from $500,000 and up.

Trade and Industry References

There are literally hundreds of directories that list organizations in specialized fields. To name them all would be impossible and to name just a few would be misleading. All areas of interest are covered by a directory of some kind which will list the organizations that participate in that activity. The basic directories will suggest what references to consult in researching your area of interest. If you have difficulty locating what you want, contact someone already in the business for suggestions as to where it might be found.

You might also check with professional associations active in your field of interest. Two publications with listings of professional associations are: *Career Guide to Professional Associations: A Directory of Organizations by Occupational Fields* (The Carroll Press, 43 Squantum Street, Cranston, R.I.) and *Encyclopedia of Associations* (Gale Research Company, Book Tower, Detroit, Michigan).

Regional Directories

If you are confining your search for a job to a specific area of the country you will find that there are directories and publications that list business organizations in that region. There are directories for cities, counties, and states. Contact the Chamber of Commerce serving the locality in which you are interested for local listings.

Larger areas are covered by such publications as the *New England Directory of Manufacturers* (George D. Hall Company, 20 Kilby Street, Boston, Massachusetts). Names and addresses of manufacturing companies within the six state region are listed along with locations of branches, products, principal officers, and number of employees. Similar directories are published for all regions or states.

Probably the best all-inclusive regional directory published is the *Yellow Pages* of the Telephone Directory. Here you will find every organization in the area listed alphabetically and grouped by product manufactured or service rendered.

Special Resources for College Graduates

There are a number of special publications prepared specifically for college students and graduates which are distributed free of charge on many campuses. Check with your placement office for availability on your campus. Among them are:

College Placement Annual (College Placement Council Inc., P.O. Box 2263, Bethlehem, Pa.). United States and Canadian organizations which regularly hire college graduates are listed alphabetically, cross-indexed by occupation and geography. Each brief listing includes information on the openings available, and gives the name, title and address of the proper person to contact.

Business World Men and *Business World Women* (University Communications, Inc., 37 W. Cherry Street, Rahway, N.J.). Published three times a year, these magazines contain articles on a wide variety of careers for college seniors. They also contain a Directory of Public Corporations. Included are the names of the 100 largest industrial corporations, 10 largest retailing companies, 10 largest utilities, 10 largest commercial banks, 10 largest diversified financial companies and 15 largest life insurance companies.

Affirmative Action Register (Affirmative Action, Inc., 8356 Olive Boulevard, St. Louis, Missouri). Issued monthly, this publication contains advertisements of professional and managerial positions throughout the country for female, minority and handicapped candidates.

Ways to Contact Employers

All business organizations must seek new personnel from time to time in order to replace members of their staff who resign or retire, or to provide new manpower to handle increased demands because of growth of the business. Providing this new manpower is vital to the success of any organization. Large companies maintain sizable staffs and spend considerable sums to attract and hire new workers. A company may use one, or several avenues to attract applicants, and the avenues used may vary considerably from one type of business to another and among various businesses in the same field. Knowledge of the methods that companies most often use to recruit college graduates is important to your job campaign. The serious careerist will not confine himself to one method, but will use several in order to increase the possibility of finding the perfect job.

College recruiting program. Every year, several hundred companies send recruiters to campuses all over the country for the purpose of interviewing college seniors for possible employment. By participating in the "recruiting program", you can learn about opportunities with many companies in a minimum amount of time. It will probably be the only time in your life when so many companies come seeking you, rather than your having to seek out the company. While the majority of recruiters are seeking applicants with technical background, an increasing number are showing an interest in the non-technical graduate. Check with your college placement office for details of the recruiting program on your campus.

College placement office. Even though your college may not operate a recruiting program, all colleges do provide some kind of placement service for their graduating seniors and alumni. Employers have found this service to be an excellent source of manpower and will contact the office whenever they have openings. An active placement office will also maintain continuing contact with employers interested in recruiting college-trained personnel. Through this contact they may be able to provide good leads for job opportunities even though open requisitions for candidates may not be on file.

In addition, your placement office maintains a library which may contain some of the directories mentioned earlier in this chapter, as well as literature prepared by companies specifically for college graduates describing their business, job opportunities and employment advantages. The importance of the college placement office to the efforts of the careerist trying to locate a meaningful job cannot be overemphasized.

(A thorough discussion of college recruiting programs and college placement facilities is offered in Chapter Five.)

Professors and Deans. Through their active participation in professional associations and consulting, faculty members have wide contacts with employers in their field of specialty. Some employers, particularly in highly specialized fields, may prefer to use this method of recruiting college-trained personnel because of the detailed personal recommendations that the faculty member can make.

Private employment agencies. Many companies prefer to use this source of manpower. Since private agencies must produce results in order to stay in business, they are very active in locating employment opportunities for applicants and candidates for job openings. A reliable agency will screen out unqualified applicants and refer only those candidates who meet the requirements of the job. This can be of advantage to you since it may save hours of time better spent on efforts more likely to produce positive results.

If you decide to contact a private employment agency a word of caution is advised. Most agencies specialize in certain types of placements, so you should determine which agencies are most active in your area of interest. Usually, a private employment agency will ask you to sign a contract that will stipulate a fee to be paid if they are successful in locating an opportunity for you which you accept. Sometimes this fee will be paid by the employer so you should determine in advance who assumes this liability.

State employment offices. Not all state employment offices handle referrals for professional help but those in the larger cities sometimes provide very effective service. This potential source of job leads should be investigated.

Trade associations and professional societies. Practically every type of business or service activity has a trade association or professional society concerned with the specialized activities of its members. Almost all of them have a publication of some kind in which there will be listings of positions available. Also, these same publications carry position-wanted listings where you may place an ad, often free of charge, that will bring your qualifications to the attention of potential employers. National and regional meetings of professional societies are very often excellent places to make contacts. In addition, many local chapters run active placement programs, acting as a clearing house for job candidates and employers.

Newspapers. Everyone is familiar with the classified advertising section of newspapers. During your job campaign, a daily scanning of the help wanted listings is highly recommended. Most large city dailies not only carry listings for local opportunities, but also many listings for jobs in other parts of the country. Newspapers with extremely wide circulation, such as the *Wall Street Journal* or the *New York Times* can be particularly helpful.

Direct application. Perhaps, after you have studied your interests and qualifications and your research has produced a list of companies that you are interested in contacting, a direct approach is called for. A letter or a telephone call is an excellent way to bring yourself to the attention of an employer. The use of letters to obtain interviews with specific companies will be discussed in detail in the next chapter.

Following the steps and suggestions outlined in this chapter may seem tedious and unnecessary, but it is time well spent. It may save you the unhappiness and frustration of being in the wrong career, and the cost of having to start all over again in a new direction. Next to choosing a mate, career selection is the most important decision you will probably be called upon to make in your lifetime.

A well organized job campaign should result in several excellent offers of employment and you will be in the happy position of judging which of these several offers will be most advantageous to your development. Don't be stampeded into making selections without facts. The higher than average salary offer may be made by a desperate employer who needs personnel in order to meet a contract deadline, and who will no longer need your services once that deadline has been met. The glamorous sounding title may be a cover-up for very routine responsibilities. Arm yourself with as much information as you can gather and choose wisely.

Chapter Seven

BASIC TOOLS: RESUMES and LETTERS

by

Sidney F. Austin

A salesman must find a customer who wants his product in order to make a sale. Similarly, you must find an employer who wants your services in order to secure a position. You and the salesman will use the same techniques in order to realize your respective objectives not the least of which is a sound advertising campaign; letting the customer know about the qualities of the product available. In your own case you are the product, a combination of personality, ability, and experience which you will present to your potential customers; employers who can use what you have to offer.

YOUR RESUME

The most important tool in your advertising kit, and an indispensable part of your job campaign, is your resume. Known variously as a personal data sheet, a personal profile, or a qualification record, the resume is a digest of your qualifications for a job. Since it is prepared by you to be used by you, it is your distinctive advertising brochure. This quality of distinctiveness is what makes a good resume so valuable.

Your resume allows you to present yourself to a potential employer as you want to be seen. Almost always, a resume is required either for an interview and in many cases before an interview. No job search should begin until your resume is ready.

Content of a Resume

Your resume is made up of many parts, some necessary and some optional. How much information about yourself you will eventually include in your resume will be a matter of individual choice. Since authorities do not agree on the necessity of including the information called for under some of the following headings they will be identified as optional.

As each section is discussed, write down everything called for under that particular heading. The decision as to what to include and what to drop will come later as you construct your final draft.

Identification

Your name, address and telephone number identifies your resume and would appear as the first item on it. You will have to decide whether to include both your school and home addresses and telephone numbers or whether one will suffice. The answer will depend on the timing of your campaign and whether you can be more easily contacted at one or the other.

Professional Objective (Optional)

A statement as to your professional objective is a highly effective resume tool but it can also limit its effective use. Employers will be impressed by an applicant who knows what he wants; but if you are still considering alternate career choices, a statement naming a specific job will severely limit the use of your resume.

If you decide to include a statement of objective on your resume, use as specific a title as possible without being too restrictive. Tie the title in with some field of work. For example —

> Production management position in a manufacturing firm in the metal working field
>
> Community worker or organizer in community-oriented programs.

Also consider a statement such as the following which not only states the type of job being sought but includes justification for the request. Of course the resume must support the claim of experience to which it refers.

Civil Engineering graduate seeks challenging position with a consulting firm. Familiar with design and construction techniques in the heavy construction field.

Personal Data (Optional)

Included in this section are identifying items such as date of birth, height, weight, health and marital status including number of children, if any. This information can be arranged in a paragraph but is usually arranged in block form, lending itself to easy scanning by the reader. Other items such as special skills or important hobbies may be included here or you may wish to include them under a separate heading, *Activities and Interests*, which is discussed later in this chapter.

Educational Background

Your listing of educational achievements begins with your most advanced training, followed by a listing in inverse order, of all other schools attended.

The names of all colleges or universities you have attended should be listed along with their locations, dates of attendance, degrees (to be) received, and major and minor courses of study including options, if any. The titles of significant projects or your thesis may be included as well as the names of any honors or awards you have received. You may wish to give your quality point average, or better yet, your class rank but only if you rank in the top quarter of your class. Public disclosure of a lower ranking does not help and may hurt your cause.

You may include information concerning your involvement in extracurricular activities under each school listing or you may wish to include this information under *Activities and Interests.* Read that section and consider your own situation before you decide.

If you have been in one of the military services, list service schools attended including dates of attendance and the extent of your training.

Listing the high school you attended is not necessary. Do so only if you feel your record there will be helpful in selling yourself to an employer. Since your latest achievements are your most important, a good college record makes an outstanding high school record relatively insignificant.

Work Experience

Any work that you have ever done, including part-time or summer jobs, could be of interest to an employer and can be used to illustrate your skills and qualifications. The extent to which you will be offering a complete work history to an employer will depend on the amount of experience you have to offer. Employers will be chiefly interested in your most recent experience so you should give it the most attention, however any experience significant to the field of your current interest should receive equally important treatment.

List each job giving the name and location of each employer, dates of employment, job title, and a description of your duties. The description of the duties of each job should be in paragraph form giving particular emphasis to tasks performed, indicating specialties learned, skills that were developed, scope of responsibility, to whom you were responsible, and results achieved. These descriptions should be concise, but informative. Of particular significance are experiences illustrating leadership potential, organizational ability, communication skills, ingenuity, and teamwork. You should include all experiences back to the time you graduated from high school.

This section of your resume is not easy to write, and because of its importance deserves considerable time and effort. At a later time, after you have decided on a format which will dictate the way in which your material will be presented, you will be called upon to reduce your descriptions to their essential information.

Military Service

If you have been on active duty with any of the armed services, list your branch, dates of service, highest rank achieved, duties, assignments and responsibilities. If your responsibilities were significant to your vocational objective, you could include this experience in the *Work Experience* section.

Activities and Interests (Optional)

Whether or not you include a separate section in your resume to include items under this heading depends on the number of items that you have to offer. Items of potential interest to an employer that could be included here are memberships in professional and honorary societies, school organizations and activities, titles of articles or papers that you have presented or have had published, skills you have learned, discoveries or inventions credited to you, special licenses you possess, community activities and involvement, foreign language proficiency, and hobbies. If you have held office in any of your activities or have been appointed chairman of an important committee, be sure to mention the fact.

As an alternative to a separate heading for the information to be included here, you could put skills and hobbies in the *Personal Data* section of your resume and your extracurricular activities under your college or university listing in the *Educational Background* section.

References

It is not necessary or desirable to list references on your resume although you should include a statement that "References will be furnished upon request." If asked, supply the names, titles, and appropriate addresses of those people whom you feel will be particularly helpful to you for the job you are trying to get. Have several names available so that no one person will have to bear the burden of commenting on your qualifications to several potential employers.

It goes without saying that you should not give anyone's name as your reference without receiving his or her permission to do so. A surprise request for information about you could be resented, resulting in unfavorable comments. Your references should also receive a copy of your resume.

Among those whom you might consider as a reference, you should include someone who is familiar with your educational accomplishments such as a professor or a dean; someone who is familiar with your work capabilities such as a co-worker or a work supervisor; and someone who will testify as to your character. Clergymen or politicians are not considered to be good candidates as references except in their respective fields, since it is generally felt that they will not be objective about your qualifications. Classmates and relatives are definitely not acceptable.

Format of a Resume

Your next step in the preparation of your resume is to select a format approach that you feel will do the best job of presenting your qualifications. The type of approach that you use will, to some extent, dictate the typographical layout of your resume and is dependent on what items in your background you wish to emphasize.

The most important element of most college students' qualifications is the education they are receiving. For this reason many of you would feature your educational background by placing it in a prominent position on your resume. Or you might have had an opportunity to acquire some meaningful vocational experience which would interest potential employers. Consider the various approaches, take a look at the sample resumes, and decide for yourself how you want your resume to read and look.

Historical Approach   *(See Figure 1)*

The historical approach assumes that your most recent activity is your most important and emphasizes this fact by placing it in a primary position on your resume. Whether you feature your education or your experience by putting one section before the other, listings under each heading are placed in inverse chronological order starting with your most recent schooling and your most recent job. Dates are included to show the length of each experience.

Most resumes circulating today use this format. Employers find it easy to follow because its logical sequence allows them to trace easily your educational and experience history. This approach is also well suited to the job seeker with limited experience.

In constructing an historical type of resume, care must be taken to avoid letting your significant experiences get lost in the details of dates, trivial jobs, and unessential facts.

Functional Approach   *(See Figure 2)*

The functional type of resume emphasizes the function, or title, of the jobs you have held, with the most significant being placed in the most prominent position. Impressive job titles you have held and responsible duties you have performed are featured to support your qualifications for the type of job you are seeking. Names of employers and dates of employment, although they are included in the descriptions, are subordinated to function.

Experienced individuals might find this approach to the resume extremely useful. A functional approach might also allow you to feature part-time or temporary work in your career field more effectively than the historical approach.

Analytical Approach (See Figure 3)

The analytical approach allows the job seeker even more flexibility than the functional approach in that particular vocational skills or specialized knowledge may be featured by grouping background experience regardless of where the experience was gained. Historical sequence is ignored as elements of training and experience from several sources are grouped to show their applicability to your career goal.

You would list your schools and employers, giving job titles and dates, but this list need not be complete as far as covering every experience you may have been exposed to nor does it need to be featured on your resume.

An analytical type of resume will help the applicant who has had frequent job changes to minimize these changes. Also the applicant who wishes to change the direction of his career may find that the analytical approach will allow him to demonstrate more effectively how his background can be applied to his new goals.

Imaginative Approach (See Figure 4)

One other approach, using an imaginative format, should be mentioned. The "imaginative" resume may be an adaptation of any of the other approaches or it may be entirely original.

Layout of the resume need not follow any of the established rules, allowing you to draw attention to specific qualifications by using display techniques. You could include quotations from favorable comments by teachers or supervisors. Attention-getting headlines might be employed. Particular qualifications might be underlined or enclosed in a box for emphasis.

The imaginative type of resume is tricky to construct and will not be appreciated in many fields so its use is limited. Employers in art, advertising, or journalism—fields in which originality of expression is a premium—might be impressed, but many other employers could be annoyed. When in doubt, a more conservative approach is safest.

Layout and Language of a Resume

After you have decided which type of format is best suited to your purpose, your next consideration is the physical layout of your material on the page and the language that is used to present it. It should be kept in mind that a resume is not a complete history of a person's background but a very specialized capsule of the significant aspects of that background which qualifies the person for consideration by an employer. Your resume must be concise and to the point, easy to read, and pleasing to the eye.

Here are a number of suggestions to keep in mind as you write your final draft.

1.   Your resume should be confined to one page if possible. Very few college students have had enough experience to justify more than that. If you are one

of those few, however, do not hesitate to use the space you need to tell your story but do not go beyond two pages.

2.   Experiment with the arrangement of headlines, captions, and text so as to find the best total appearance and readability. Use capital letters and underlining sparingly. Use indentation as a means of identifying separate items.

3.   Balance the material on the page so that the total effect is pleasing to the eye. Leave sufficient margins so that the page does not look crowded. Fill the page, so as not to leave excessive space at the bottom.

4.   Be consistent in the use of graphic display techniques. Do not use indentation in one section and underscoring in the next.

5.   As you edit your material keep in mind your intended purpose. Eliminate unimportant details. Stress accomplishments you are proud of. Write and rewrite until you are satisfied that your descriptions are factual, positive statements of your experience, giving promise of potential continued growth.

6.   You may write in complete sentences or splinters of sentences as long as your meaning is clear. The test is whether your text is readable and understandable. Use simple words that convey exactly the meaning you intend. Use punctuation marks intelligently.

7.   It is not necessary to use the first person pronoun unless the text does not make sense without it. Since you are writing about yourself, verbs imply the "I" as subject. Use of the third person in referring to yourself is not acceptable unless contained in a quotation by another person.

8.   Use present tense in referring to activities in which you are currently engaged, but anything previous to current activity must be referred to in past tense.

9.   Use skill/action words in describing your duties and responsibilities to show what you have done. (Example: designed, implemented, performed, etc.)

10.   Avoid the use of slang, professional jargon and trite expressions. Do not abbreviate. Employers who must take the time to interpret what you are saying will probably not bother.

11.   Consult a dictionary for correct spellings. Mistakes reflect on your education, and therefore your qualifications.

12.   Before you type your final copy have someone else give you his reaction to it. Your family and friends, or your school placement officer may be able to offer helpful suggestions. Consider your own reaction after setting it aside for a day or two. Would you hire the person described in this resume?

It would be too time-consuming to type individually more than a very few copies of your resume and it would be too expensive to pay to have it done. Offset printing, also known as multilith, is a recommended means of reproducing copies and there are many outfits with the facilities to provide this service. Mimeograph is also acceptable if it is done carefully. Spirit process or electrostatic copying are less desirable because of the difficulty of producing copies of uniform quality.

The sample resumes shown are examples only. Consider the different approaches, layouts, and language. Experiment with your own ideas. Your resume should truly represent you.

YOUR LETTER OF APPLICATION

Whenever you send a resume to an employer in answer to an advertisement or some other lead, it must be accompanied by a letter of transmittal, better known as a letter of application. A letter of application is an absolute essential if you plan to conduct a job campaign using the direct application method. The purpose of this letter is to introduce yourself to the employer by telling him why you are writing to him and what contribution you believe you can make to his organization based on your qualifications, and to ask him to take the action necessary to arrange an interview so that your qualifications may be reviewed in light of his needs.

Letters of application fall into two categories depending on the type of mail campaign you are conducting. These two categories are called the "rifle" approach and the "shotgun" approach. You would send a "rifle" type of letter when you are investigating a specific job lead or possibility. You may be answering an advertisement or following up on a suggestion offered by your college placement office, one of your professors, or a friend. The nature of the opening is known and you would construct your letter to show how your abilities can be applied to meet the employer's needs.

The "shotgun" type letter is necessarily less specific. Research into your field of interest has produced the names of many employers who might be able to offer you the kind of work you have decided to do. However, you have no way of knowing if these employers are currently looking for help. Through the use of a letter, you present your qualifications to these organizations in the hope that they will be interested enough to consider you for possible employment.

Your intended purpose with either type of letter is the same: to obtain an interview. Although few employers will hire an applicant without a personal interview, an initial favorable impression created by a good letter of application can increase your chances of success. It is not easy to write a good letter, which is why a good one can be effective. Carefully prepared, your letter will stand out and your application will receive more than casual consideration.

The biggest mistake that most letter writers make is to approach the task from their own point of view. You are writing because you are looking for a job. The employer knows this as well as you do, so why waste time telling him so. Use your time to tell him things he wants to know about you. Tell him how your abilities could be a real benefit to him or to his company. Don't put the emphasis on what you have done but rather on what you can do because of what you have done. Offer a service, show how you can make good on that offer, then ask for an interview.

Your letter of application is a business letter and should follow all the rules of layout and format of a business letter. Even before he begins reading, the employer will begin to form an impression of you by what he sees. This impression will be favorable if the letter is neat and well laid out on good stationery. Margins must be even, and the letter should be well balanced on the page from top to bottom.

Address your letter to a specific individual in the company. Who are you trying to reach? Is it the sales manager, the vice president of manufacturing, or the personnel director? The name of the person you want to reach is probably available in your placement office or in a directory. As a last resort, you might telephone the company and ask the switchboard operator for the correct name and title.

Content of a Letter of Application

The first paragraph in your letter should be composed so as to attract attention and a favorable interest in you on the part of the reader. It should tell why you are writing the letter and it should raise questions about you in the mind of the reader so that he will be encouraged to know you better.

"During the past year I have read of several announcements of promotions within your company, including your own. Investigation has revealed that your company is expanding rapidly because you produce outstanding products and supply excellent service to your customers. I would like to be a part of your dynamic organization and believe I can help materially in maintaining your reputation."

This candidate has created attention by referring to something the company is proud of, the rapid growth of their business. He ends by offering his services to help them maintain this growth. The reader is encouraged to find out what this candidate has to offer.

Another way to create attention and interest is to refer to someone with whom both you and the reader are mutually acquainted.

"Mr. John Simpson, one of your accountants, has suggested that I write you concerning my qualifications for an opening in his department. John's obvious enthusiasm for his job is contagious and has created a desire on my part to share the same enthusiasm."

The two examples shown above are typical of opening paragraphs which are appropriate for "rifle" type letters. You will have to use a more general approach for your lead paragraph in a "shotgun" type of letter.

"Successful experiences with electronic equipment manufacturers during my cooperative work assignments while attending Northeastern University and a heavy emphasis on the use of computers to solve engineering problems presented in class have created a desire on my part to work for a manufacturer of digital computer equipment. A leader in this field, your company offers the kind of atmosphere where my background can be applied to our mutual benefit."

All of these opening paragraphs, while differing greatly in style and content, have one thing in common. They tell the reader why he is writing to him and offer a reason why he should consider your application further. They also appeal to the reader's self-interest.

Now your task is to justify his interest in your candidacy by emphasizing your qualifications for the job for which you are applying. Your approach must be positive, presenting applicable items in your background to prove your potential value to his company. Don't waste time commenting on or apologizing for weaknesses. Use specific examples to make your point. Don't go into great detail and don't introduce material that is not immediately relevant to the purpose of the letter. You may refer the reader to your resume for miscellaneous details of your qualifications. Your objective in these middle paragraphs is to create a desire on the part of the reader to invite you in for an interview.

The following paragraphs might be written by a candidate who is short on vocational experience in his chosen field, but who makes the most of what background he possesses. A candidate with vocational experience would similarly show how his qualifications can be applied. State positively what kind of job you are interested in. Don't force the employer to make this decision because he may not bother.

"During my attendance at Midwest University, I worked on the campus newspaper as a reporter, was promoted to Managing Editor, and in my senior year, served as Editor-in-Chief. These positions gave me experience in interviewing people to get the facts for an article, writing feature stories and columns, directing the efforts of others to produce articles of interest, and deciding on the content and format of each issue. I believe this experience can be of assistance to your organization in your public relations department."

"I have been active in campus organizations and have always enjoyed good relations with my classmates and professors. You may refer to my enclosed resume for additional details of my qualifications for a position with your company."

The writer of the foregoing paragraph has done his job quickly and well. He has created a desire on the part of the reader to know more about him by relating his background to a possible opening and by showing how this background can be useful to the company.

Having created a desire to know about you, it is time to close the letter by asking for a response. Your request should be specific and positive and ask for action. Suggest a day or week when you will be available for an interview. A vague closing expressing hope for a response is poor psychology.

"I will be available for an interview during the week of March 9 and would like to talk with you at that time. Please let me know what day would be most convenient for you."

Close your letter with a formal salutation. "Very truly yours," "Sincerely yours," or "Yours sincerely" are acceptable forms. "Sincerely" is too personal and "Respectfully yours" is outmoded. Type your name three spaces below the salutation, then add your signature. If you include an enclosure with your letter such as your resume, type "Enclosure" below your signature even with the left-hand margin of your letter.

Set-Up of a Letter of Application

Figure 5 shows the layout of a good letter. The format shown is the one most commonly used, although there are other acceptable forms. Follow the style discussed and you should have an effective letter which may be used as a model, revised only to fit the circumstances of each individual application. Specific examples of words to use in a letter of application have been deliberately kept to a minimum. Using a sample letter presented in a textbook and substituting your qualifications in the proper places will result in a letter that appears to have been constructed that way. Use your imagination and write sincerely. After all, it is you who is writing the letter and you should appear in it.

Don't expect 100 per cent response from your letters and don't expect 100 per cent results from the responses you do get. A 50 per cent response would be considered excellent and a percentage of these will be courtesy replies with no invitation to an interview. Even if your letter may not immediately lead to an interview it still may have been worth the effort. Many employers file applications that they are interested in for future reference when an opening for which the candidate may be qualified may develop.

BIBLIOGRAPHY

Calvert, Robert, Jr. and Steele, John E. *Planning Your Career.* N.Y., Mc-Graw Hill Book Co., Inc. 1963.

Carroll Press Staff. *Career Guide to Professional Associations: A Directory of Organizations by Occupational Field.* Second Edition. Cranston, R.I., The Carroll Press, 1980.

Edlund, Sidney and Edlund, Mary. *Pick Your Job and Land it.* Englewood Cliffs, N. J., Prentice-Hall, Inc., 1954.

Gates, James E. and Miller, Harold. *Personal Adjustment to Business.* Englewood Cliffs, N. J., Prentice-Hall, Inc., 1958.

Lowen, Walter. *You and Your Job.* N. Y., Collier Books, 1962.

Nutter, Carolyn F. *The Resume Workbook: A Personal Career File for Job Applications.* Fifth edition. Cranston, R.I., The Carroll Press, 1978.

(Figure 1 — Historical Approach)

MARY ANN EVANS
1121 Massachusetts Avenue
Cambridge, Massachusetts 02139
(617) 555-2110

PERSONAL DATA

Date of Birth: October 18, 1958   Marital Status: Single
Height: 5 ft., 7 in.   Health: Excellent
Weight: 130 lbs.

EDUCATION

Northeastern University, Boston, Massachusetts   June, 1980
     Bachelor of Arts Degree in Mathematics, Minor in Physics

Cambridge High and Latin School, Cambridge Massachusetts
     College Preparatory Course   June, 1975

EXTRA-CURRICULAR ACTIVITIES

Society of Women Engineers, Recording Secretary-Treasurer 3, 4, President, 5; Yacht Club, Secretary-Treasurer 3, 4; Dean of Women's Advisory Board; Senior Week Committee; Varsity Cheerleader.

WORK EXPERIENCE

AVCO-Everett Research Laboratory, Everett, Massachusetts.
     Computing Department (Coop) 1977-1980. Provided computational support of the differential type for Error Analysis Report of the Calibration Group. Operated in Dial-Data and Telcomp shared time computer system formats. Made analysis of data used in re-entry experiments. Programmed IBM 360/44 Computer in Fortran IV language. Reduced shock tube data and made mathematical analyses in support of Plasma Physics Research. Programmed EAI 3500 Data Plotter. Revised and submitted various programs.

John Hancock Mutual Life Insurance Co., Boston, Massachusetts.
     Personnel Research Department (Coop) 1976-1977. Researched data and compiled statistics on various projects including Personnel Testing. Updated statistics on absence and termination reports. Prepared data and graphs for publication. Maintained statistical files.

REFERENCES

References will be furnished upon request.

(Figure 2 — Functional Approach)

FRANK JONES
423 North Allen Street
Medford, Massachusetts 02346
(617) 555-4180

PROFESSIONAL OBJECTIVE

To obtain an Industrial Engineering position offering both Potential for growth and the opportunity to experience all facets of Industrial Engineering.

PROFESSIONAL EXPERIENCE

INDUSTRIAL ENGINEER

International Business Machines Corporation.
Poughkeepsie, New York, 1978-1980.
— Supported vendorization of manufacturing operations from the Poughkeepsie plant.
  Generated workload and space requirements.
  Designed layout of vendorization support areas.
  Determined vendorization costs.
  Coordinated twelve internal functions involving work scheduling and organization of status meetings.
— Provided industrial engineering support of manufacturing department for operating plan, including work load and space.
— Supplied internal logistics support for parts and assemblies.
— Implemented a program to aid in parts disbursement and storage.
— Designed and implemented a simulation model which tracked the utilization of internal movement equipment. Program results led to actions which enabled the site to meet an increased schedule.

SUPERVISOR

Popular Services Incorporated, Passaic, New Jersey, 1976-1977.
— Developed incentive program production standards by stopwatch time-study methods.
— Defined and instituted company procedures.
— Supervised sixteen person Computer Output Corrections Department.
— Supervised twenty-two person Christmas Refund Unit. Responsibility included hiring, training and scheduling.

EDUCATION

Bachelor of Science degree in industrial engineering, Northeastern University, Boston, Mass., June, 1980.
— Member of American Institute of Industrial Engineers, student chapter.
— Member of Judo Club; participated in tournament competition.
— Experience gained through Northeastern's cooperative education program.

INTERESTS

Participatory team sports, photography, silk screening, backpacking, travel, gourmet cooking.

REFERENCES

References will be furnished on request.

(Figure 3 — Analytical Approach)

BRUCE H. BAKER
125 Maple Avenue
Hicksville, New York 11801
(516) 555-6142

Vocational Objective

Management Service Trainee in a public accounting firm.

Qualifications

Accounting experience. B.S. degree in Accounting, June, 1980.
Six months experience as a junior accountant with a Certified Public Accountant working on certified reports, audits, and the preparation of corporation taxes. payroll taxes, and state and federal income tax returns. Three months experience in the Comptrollers Department of a large bank working on the daily balance sheet, with responsibility for monthly statements on demand and time deposits.

Financial experience. Twelve months of experience in the handling of securities in the Customer Securities Department of a large bank and with a securities broker. Gained knowledge in the operation of the stock exchange.

(Attended Northeastern University, Boston, Massachusetts, where the above experience was gained on cooperative education assignments. Participated in student government, club and professional activities. Ranked in top quarter of class.)

Employers

Robert T. Walker, C.P.A., Glen Cove, New York
Junior Staff Accountant   June — December, 1979

Marine Midland Grace Trust Company, New York, N.Y.
Accounting Trainee   March, 1978 — March, 1979

Bache and Company, New York, N.Y.
Junior Securities Clerk   December, 1976 — December, 1977

Personal Information

Single, excellent health, 6 ft. 1 in., 185 pounds.
Born April 3, 1956. Will furnish references on request.

(Figure 4 – Imaginative Approach)

LILLIAN F. SIMMONS
24 Warren Street
Arlington, Mass. 02174
Tel. (617) 555-3405

"As long as I can remember, I have wanted to be a Social Worker."

Consider My Qualifications

education 1980	NORTHEASTERN UNIVERSITY — Boston, Mass. B.A. in Sociology (5-year Cooperative Education Program) Honors received: Freshman Honor List; Dean's List 2, 3, 4, 5; Alpha Kappa Delta (Sociology Honor Society) 4, 5; The Academy (Liberal Arts Honor Society) 4, 5.
1975	ARLINGTON HIGH SCHOOL — Arlington, Mass. College Preparatory Course
work experience dec 1978 to dec 1979	WESTBOROUGH STATE HOSPITAL — Westborough, Mass. Case Aide (Cooperative Education Assignment) Provided assistance and services as prescribed for individual cases by social workers. Made placement and pre-placement visits to the community; jobs, nursing homes and rest homes. Formulated admission notes, initial social work plans, progress notes and placement notes. Provided short term non-intensive service to patients and relatives. Did initial interviews for Medicaid. Led therapy group with geriatric patients.
sept 1977 to june 1978	JOHN HANCOCK MUTUAL LIFE INSURANCE CO. — Boston. Retirement Clerk-Calculator (Coop. Education Assignment) Calculated pension benefits. Coded and recorded retirements. Calculated death benefits.
dec 1976 to sept 1977	DECISIONS SCIENCE LABORATORY — Bedford, Mass. Project Assistant (Cooperative Education Assignment) Reduced and edited data from psychological testing. Typed data onto computer tape. Participated in various psychological tests.
activities and interests	Northeastern Hus-skiers and Outing Club 1, 2, 3; Silver Masque (Dramatic Club) 1, 2, 3; Sociology Club 3, 4, 5; Delta Pi Alpha Sorority 2, 3, 4, 5; Swimming; Tennis.
personal	single 5 feet 8 inches 140 pounds excellent health
references	References will be furnished upon request.

Figure 5

Your Street Address
City, State, Zip
Today's Date

Mr. Paul W. Alexander
Personnel Manager
Allen Manufacturing Company
185 Broad Street
Stamford, Conn. 06901

Dear Mr. Alexander:

Your opening paragraph should <u>arouse interest</u> on the part of the reader. Tell him why you are writing the letter. Give information to show your specific interest in his company.

Your middle paragraphs should <u>create desire</u>. Give details of your background that will show the reader why he should consider you as a candidate. Be as specific as possible about the kind of job you want. Don't make the reader try to guess what you would be interested in.

Refer the reader to your general qualifications on your enclosed resume or other material. Use as much space as you need to tell your story but keep it brief and to the point.

In your closing paragraph you <u>ask for action</u>. Ask for an appointment suggesting a time when you will be free. A positive request is harder to ignore than a vague hope.

Very truly yours,

Ronald E. Brown

Enclosure

Chapter Eight

THE INTERVIEW

by

Sidney F. Austin

The moment of truth in your job campaign is the interview. It is the final step that must be taken in order to secure the position you are seeking. You will be offering your education, your experience, and your personality to an employer who might offer you the opportunity to gain new experience, build a reputation, and start a career. The interview is crucially important to both you and the employer because it is the best way for each to determine what the other has to offer. The serious careerist should be suspicious of the organization that would be willing to employ hime or her without asking him or her to justify in person his/her right to employment.

The interview has been described as a "mutual exchange of information." Its objectives are: to supply information about you to the employer that is not contained in your resume or on an application blank, and to enable him to evaluate your personality in terms of the demands of the company or a possible position; to enable you to gain additional information about the company not available in published materials; and to give you and the employer an opportunity to discuss the desirability of further contact, or possibly an offer of employment.

Before the Interview

Many companies hire only five to ten per cent of all the applicants they interview. While it is true that the ratio of offers extended would be somewhat higher—not all applicants receiving an offer will accept it—these figures indicate that interviewing is a serious business and deserves more than casual preparation. It is not enough to merely show up for an interview and present yourself for analysis and evaluation. You must be an active participant in the "exchange" and be as ready to ask questions as you are to answer them. Before you step into the employer's office, you must acquire the self-confidence necessary to make a good impression and self-confidence can only be gained by knowing you are ready.

How much do you know about the company you are trying to get a job with? Do you know what the company makes or what service it performs? Do you know how large the organization is and the principal locations? Do you know anything about the person who will be interviewing you?

If you have answers to these questions, it will do wonders for your self-confidence. You will be regarded as a person who has a sincere interest in the company because you have taken the time to find out something about it. You will be able to ask intelligent questions during the interview which will be regarded as further evidence of your interest.

Companies that recruit college graduates prepare an information sheet which contains pertinent facts about the company. If your college placement office does not have this information, the company will be happy to send it to you at your request. Also, much information can be gained by checking the reference material suggested in   a preceding chapter.

Just as important as knowledge of the company is knowledge of yourself. Don't wait for the interview to try to think of a coherent response to the question, "Tell me about yourself." This is not an infrequent opener for an interview and the effectiveness of your answer will help to determine whether it turns out to be successful.

You would do well to rehearse what you want to say during the interview, but don't prepare a speech and memorize it. Decide ahead of time what you will say if you are asked about previous experience, why you are leaving your present job or why you left your last job, and why you are applying for this job. You will find it much easier to make a good impression if you are able to talk swiftly, clearly and coherently.

Your feeling of self-confidence will be enhanced if you know that you look right, that you present an attractive appearance. First impressions are lasting impressions and valuable interview time may be spent attempting to overcome an initial negative reaction. An applicant seeking a professional position is expected to look like a professional. You simply won't get fair consideration unless you do.

Men should wear a suit, clean shirt and a tie. Their shoes must be shined and they must have a clean shave and a neat haircut. Women must dress in good taste and use a minimum of make-up. Both should appear neat, clean, well-dressed, and conservative. While casual clothes might be accepted by some interviewers, is the possible loss of a good job worth the self-satisfaction of showing your independence of custom?

During the Interview

Being late for an interview is inexcusable, so be sure that you arrive for your appointment on time, even earlier if possible. The person you are going to see is probably on a tight schedule. If you are late you not only create a bad initial impression but the time lost will be subtracted from the time allotted to you. If you are early and the interviewer is ahead of schedule, you may find you have extra time to sell yourself.

Don't worry about being nervous as you approach the interview because this is normal behavior and will be accepted. Just remember that the interviewer is not an enemy but a friend who is anxious to hire you if you are appropriately qualified. It would be advisable, though, to dry a damp brow or a sweaty palm just before you meet.

Greet the interviewer as you enter his or her office. Many interviewers will use your first name on the theory that this will put you more at ease. Don't interpret this as meaning that you have the same privilege.

If the interviewer offers to shake your hand, do so with a firm but gentle grasp. A hand grip that is too weak or too strong makes a bad impression and gets the interview off to a poor start. Do not take the initiative yourself. Do not sit until you are invited to do so and then sit in the chair indicated. Do not smoke unless the interviewer offers you a cigarette or you have asked if you may after he lights up. Lack of a visible ash tray means "no smoking" so don't embarrass yourself by asking for one.

It should be kept in mind that the interviewer controls the interview and the applicant must respond to this control. This does not mean that the interview will be an inquisition. The interviewer is just as anxious as you are that the experience be a pleasant one for you and will try to create the proper atmosphere to give you your chance. But the burden is on you to prove you are the person to be hired. The interviewer has the responsibility of deciding whether your qualifications are acceptable and the interview will be conducted with this objective in mind.

The interviewer will ask you questions which are designed to get you to talk about your qualifications, and in so doing provide an understanding of your reasoning processes, your motives, and most importantly, your personality. Answer the questions briefly yet informatively. An applicant who says too much or too little is frustrating to interview.

Your comments should be positive and frank. Admit weaknesses in your background if you are asked a direct question, but in your answer try to mention some of your strengths. Never criticize former employers or complain about bad breaks.

You may be asked questions which you feel are too personal or irrelevant. What should you do if these questions annoy you? You could refuse to answer or express your annoyance in some other way such as answering in a disapproving tone of voice. The cost of such an attitude on your part, however, could be elimination from further consideration for the position. The interviewer may be trying to make an intelligent judgment concerning your personality and character which cannot be readily ascertained by asking the usual questions.

The interviewer might present you with a case problem and ask for an answer. Chances are the way you tackle the problem is of more interest than the solution you may come up with. Or you might be confronted with questions of an argumentative nature about your attitude toward "big business" or "big labor." These questions are designed to provide clues to your personality and your ability to work harmoniously and effectively with co-workers and superiors.

An extension of the "unusual question" technique leads to the use of the so-called "stress interview." The interviewer may deliberately try to embarrass you to watch your reaction. You may be subjected to offensive remarks or you may be faced with harrassment when you fail to find a quick solution to a complex problem. Stress interviewing is not widely used and is mentioned here only so that you will recognize it if it happens to you. It probably means that the interviewer is more than mildly interested in you as a candidate so you should keep your head and stay with the interview until you see how it comes out.

One very probable question in an interview is, "What salary do you expect?" The unprepared applicant is apprehensive because too low a figure or too high a figure may expose him as being either a fool or unrealistic. You could wind up stating that you "will accept the going rate" and that "salary is secondary to opportunity" and hope for the best.

A more realistic approach is to study current salary scales in the type of industry and/or occupation for which you are interviewing. There is a wide range of starting salaries in the various fields due partly to the training required to enter a particular profession, partly to the "prestige" of a profession, and partly to the supply of applicants relative to the number of opportunities available. Typical starting salaries in your field should have been part of your survey of the employment market before you decided on a career path. Therefore, when asked state a realistic figure and be prepared to bargain, knowing in advance the minimum you will accept before rejecting the offer.

Be alert for signs that the interview is over. The interviewer wants to give you a fair chance to present yourself and will be reluctant to terminate the conversation unless you are putting him or her seriously behind in his or her schedule. The thoughtless applicant who overstays will leave a negative impression. Thank the interviewer for taking the time to talk with you.

Before you leave, make sure the interviewer knows whether you are still interested in pursuing your application. Also make sure you know what is expected from you.

After the Interview

As soon as possible after the interview, make notes about what was discussed. Include the next steps that you should take, such as sending in a transcript of your grades or writing to indicate your continuing interest. A follow-up thank-you letter to the interviewer is a highly effective device that will mark you as conscientious and responsible. Include a question or two that you may not have thought of during the interview. The reply may contain a clue as to how seriously you are being considered.

You will be given a reasonable amount of time in order to decide whether you wish to accept a job offer. Some offers may contain a time limit, following which the offer will be withdrawn. If no time limit is stipulated, two weeks is generally considered sufficient time for you to decide on accepting or rejecting the offer. If you find it impossible to make up your mind within the time limit, you may write to the interviewer asking for an extension, but you must state why you want more time and you must be prepared to make an immediate decision if an extension cannot be granted.

All offers of employment deserve a reply. Your letter of accepting an offer should express your pleasure at receiving the opportunity and should confirm the details of the offer. Be sure to inform the employer when you intend to start work if the date has not been previously established. If you decide not to accept an offer, write a courteous letter explaining why. The employer needs to know how he measures up against other employers and, who knows, you may change your mind about working with that employer in the future and you will want to leave a favorable impression.

Summary

Go into your interview with the confidence of knowing that you are well prepared.

The interview is a voluntary meeting between two parties for a "mutual exchange of information" and either party may terminate it at any time. The initiative, during the interview however, belongs to the interviewer.

Remember that you have something to sell and the interviewer is anxious to buy. It is up to you to convince him or her that you are the person to be hired.

Use the interview to find out what you want to know about the company. You would be negligent to yourself if you didn't take the opportunity to get the information you need to make a wise decision if employment is offered.

Courtesy will produce courtesy in return. The interviewer is a human being like you, and will respond to a friendly approach.

I would like to close by quoting from a letter I received several years ago from a recent graduate. He had been a poor student and had serious doubts about finding the kind of job he wanted.

"Thought I'd notify you about the good news. I just landed an excellent paying job in this area. My assignment is in the applied mechanics group utilizing mostly theory obtained in the fluid mechanics courses at Northeastern.

"I interviewed with several companies, including those that you recommended. From these interviews I received three job offers.

"If a person can sell himself, his class rank is definitely overlooked by an interviewing organization. And this selling of oneself is enhanced by a definite method of attack, developed in the initial interviews. When baffled by a question in these interviews, the current grad must sit down afterwards and analyze the question and reason out the answer, consulting his textbooks if necessary. Thus, this question will never baffle him again.

"My final word to the young grad standing low scholastically in his class is never to shy away from a job application with any firm no matter how reputable an organization it might be. If they will grant an interview, the applicant should forget about his marks and think only of how capable he knows he is. With this attitude, employment should be his."

Chapter Nine

CAREER ADJUSTMENT and DEVELOPMENT

by

Philip W. Dunphy

Section I:

Protocol for the New Employee

For the graduate on his first full-time job, no period is more crucial or more nervous than the first few months. It is during this "breaking-in" period that the employer decides whether the new employee is valuable enough to keep and in what capacity. Often the whole future of employment with this organization rides on the first few weeks or months. A serious error at this time can limit the employee's progress: a positive impression can enhance it markedly. The first requirement is reorientation toward the goals of the employer.

The Employer's Goals

Whether the employer is or is not profit-oriented, and regardless of the product or service involved, the employee is expected to be productive. It is essential that the new employee—you—begin to think immediately in terms of "What can I contribute?" This may require a turn-about in your thinking. You no longer ask, "What can I learn?" or "What is in it for me?"

In accepting employment, you have formally or by implication signed a contract. In return for wages, you agree to expend your resources for the employer's benefit.

Learning and personal development should not be forgotten, but they must accept a secondary place. The first requirement is to do the job. In order to do the job, you must learn what the job is—beyond the brief description offered at the time of recruitment—and what your supervisor expects of you.

In most moderate to large corporations or organizations, some degree of formal orientation will be given. Small companies will approach the situation in a less formal way. Basically, however, regardless of size, the employer expects you to learn rapidly the following:

1. Basic and secondary goals (the employer's). Why does the organization exist?

2. Some organizational detail, including your place in the organization and your chain of authority and responsibility.

105

3.   Basic rules of behavior—hours, coffee breaks, reporting illnesses, overtime, dress and appearance, parking, use of the telephone, lunch hours, etc.

4.   The form of interpersonal behavior expected—degree of formality, modes of address, degree of familiarity, social expectations (if any), etc.

5.   Ground rules—safety, security, geography (location of facilities, offices, etc.), secondary responsibilities (turning off lights, closing windows, etc.).

Assuming that you apply yourself diligently to this orientation, you are now ready to join the team. You now face two big hazards, the first of which is People.

Interpersonal Relations

The vast majority of people who fail in jobs do so because they fail to relate well with others. Inability to do the work is much less important. As a matter of fact, it is a relatively rare cause of early dismissal. People make up every organization and it is people you must please if you can. At any rate, you must avoid displeasing others as much as possible.

In this respect, as a recent graduate, you suffer from significant problems. First, unless you are in a group of people who have had a great deal more education than you have had, you probably know more about many things than do your fellow workers of long experience, or so it seems to you. You need to realize right away that you also know a great deal less about many things than they do. You have a lot to learn. *The first thing to learn is not to let others find out how much you think you know.*

The reaction you stimulate among your fellow workers will be a result of your approach to them. At no point in your career is it more important to remember the golden rule: "Do unto others as you would they would do unto you—20 years from now!"

Be glad that you are a young, flexible sapling—but don't let all your sap out! Older employees have a greater commitment to the employer. They have invested time and effort in accomplishing his goals. Do not act in any way which will lead them to look on you as a threat to their security or even their tranquility.

Active participation in classes and seminars has led you to express yourself freely and with confidence. One of the most common failings is that you may do so now on your first job. This is fine, if you are asked. If not, you may learn a lot at this early stage by watching and listening.

You are in a new game. Your fellow workers are both your team mates and your competition. Watch and listen to find out which are which. Some will be both, but find which role they put first. A little time now spent observing may help you avoid the form of competition that the employer will not accept.

There are two additional rules which every employer (and employee) should remember: *Courtesy doesn't cost anything; and Kindness doesn't hurt.*

Romanticism is the Second Hazard

If you have had some experience in the general environment of your occupation, either in summer or cooperative work employment, this will not be a problem. If not, you may be in for a little shock. Things are not always what they seem. *The* second (and only *other major) reason for first job failure is an inability of the employee to accept the job for what it is rather than for what he thought it was.*

Reality testing is the psychologist's term for trying a new type of situation. In this particular test, you must pass or you will fail. Your employer expects you to ask questions relating to your work. He will often accept suggestions—sometimes eagerly. But he expects the job to be done! By you! On time! Thoroughly! In some cases he may expect the unreasonable and you may not accomplish it. Generally, however, he expects more or less reasonable results, not excuses.

In college you were spending your own money. Now your time is your employer's money. Your employer expects you to be at work on time. He expects your full time and attention. He expects you to produce for him.

Almost inevitably there will be some duties of your job which you will find distasteful. Life is like that. No one expects you to enjoy everything about your job. But the boss does expect you to perform all the duties of your job. It is a good policy, if you have not already adopted it, to do the things you like least before the things you like best. Procrastination is a luxury you cannot afford now.

Your employer is in many ways a bit of a stick-in-the mud. He or she not only expects you to do the work and do it according to his/her schedule, he or she also expects you to do it in his or her way. Now you know there is a better way. Okay, but do it the employer's way until you convince him or her your way is better. Again, caution — but not timidity is advised. The author recalls a case of an engineering graduate who was asked to calculate line impedances from data supplied. There were a number of cases involved and the engineer spent almost three days preparing the data and devising a computer program to supply the answers. About the midpoint of the third day, the supervisor stopped by to check progress. Looking at the now completely transformed data, the supervisor asked what the employee was doing. The supervisor listened raptly to a detailed explanation, nodding encouragement. After the engineer finished, the supervisor agreed to the approach, praised the ingenuity shown but asked only one question: "Why? Plus or minus 10 per cent is okay. Use your calculator. It will probably take you only three or four hours."

Often there is a better way. But, just possibly, someone has decided it isn't worth the cost in time or money or inconvenience.

If you can adapt yourself during these first few weeks, you will survive long enough to plan the next step. *You are one of several or many new faces in the organization. Without violating any of the basic ground rules, you must try to stand out as a recognizable, desirable individual.*

Image

The basic problem is one of creating the proper image. Image is a term which has been used and misused often in recent years. To some, it may have a soiled or sneaky implication. This can be true, but need not. *Your image will be the total reaction of others to you. It will be formed by your appearance, manner and performance.* The relative weight of these factors will differ according to your job. In any area of work relating to the public your employer serves, appearance and manner will be of great significance. In jobs remote from the public, performance or productivity will outrank appearance.

Appearance in image formation is variable. Some corporations have a recognizable appearance model; e.g., the gray flannel suit. If this is the case, the course of discretion is to adopt the model. Try to look as good as your boss but in such a model climate make sure your suit, shoes, etc., do not cost as much as his.

In most cases, some individuality of dress is permitted or expected. Don't overdo it. Consider the Freudian interpretation of the extremes before adopting any.

Along with dress, your appearance will depend on your apparent awareness, nervous habits, vigor, health and other factors. Without antagonizing your fellow workers or superiors, try to look awake, fit, ready. Women, as well as men, have their image, and dress norms apply. The degree of fashion here is important. Regardless of your affluence, it is unwise to dress more fashionably than your peers. Female supervisors and executives these days seldom affect old-fashioned styles. Again, as with men, look your best, but don't out-dress your superior. Make-up, hair styles, etc., also matter.

Manner relates to the way you seem to conduct yourself in all matters. *It is not only what you do but how you do it.* The rules of interpersonal relationship are important. In addition, your basic ethics and beliefs will show up in your image. Among a number of important points are:

1. *Loyalty.* Almost without exception, one of the most important aspects of your image is apparent loyalty to your employer. If he doesn't look good, make sure it's because of his actions, not yours. Back-stabbing of any kind is bad policy. Let your light shine, but focus it to illuminate your boss. Likely he'll get to like it and pull you up when he rises.

2. *Discretion.* Let all who will discuss their troubles with you but—
      (a) Don't talk to anyone about anyone else's problems or confidences, and

(b) Don't even listen to someone back-stabbing another. This policy may limit your associations, but it will keep you out of political disasters.

3.   *Tact.* Steer if you must, but don't shove. Many people will ask for your true opinion, but most don't want it—especially if it finds them lacking in perfection. If you are skilled in counseling and willing to do it, try a non-directive approach but be very, very careful. Negative criticism, however justified, or however indirectly expressed, will come back to haunt you.

4.   *Poise.* A part of the image is balance of elements which make up poise. Briefly stated, poise is "presence". It is a certain confidence, yet not blatant over-confidence. It is a certain humility without timidity. It is an ability to remain unshaken, yet still respond fully. It is gallantry and mild flirtatiousness without any trace of crudeness or lewdness. Perhaps it can be best characterized as that which distinguishes a true lady or gentleman from the pretenders in a group. Poise reflects a real inner peace. It is a great asset if you can develop it.

5.   *Honesty.* Let your conscience be firm. *Your whole future depends on your being trusted.* Once you fail in this trust, your ears will hear no more. It is far better to give undue credit to others than to be suspected of taking undue credit for yourself.

All of these necessary virtues apply to relationships outside the organization even more than to internal matters. Nothing can scotch a brilliant career faster than feedback from outside that an employee is being critical or loose in talking about the organization. If you must speak of your organization's shortcomings, speak only to your living companion and make sure your confidante speaks only to you of such things.

So be of strong heart and true. Let purity of purpose and manner light you from within and you will be seen as noble as you truly are.

Performance is not negligible, but it is often less important both initially and in the long run than are appearance and manner. Many a person has achieved great success and rank by looking and acting the part. In many more cases than you might think, outstanding performance is not a really essential factor. The reason is simple. Mediocre performance doesn't threaten the establishment. Outstanding performance does. The really creative, uniquely competent worker must, in some cases, cloak his talent. Otherwise, barring exceptional political acumen, s/he will make others — even superiors — so uncomfortable that they will strive to help him/her find a better job — fast! This may be good, but it can become a problem in time. If your light is really brilliant, you may have to shade it a little in the performance area.

On the other hand, in areas of new products or services, outstanding performance can, occasionally, overcome moderate deficiencies in appearance or manner.

The relative importance of these three elements will differ according to the job, of course. Appearance and manner are important in relation to nearness to the public and to administrative responsibilities. Performance is more important in non-customer connected specialties as well as in some phases of administration.

Performance involves getting the job done. Among the pertinent and measurable aspects of performance are punctuality, accuracy, completeness and closure.

Punctuality of course means getting the results on time. The best excuse is not nearly as valuable as an average performance. A delay of an hour on the part of one person may tie up a hundred others for a day. When the boss says "tomorrow", he doesn't mean next week. Set a schedule and stick to it. Learn to evaluate each new assignment quickly to find things that may require advance scheduling or research. Get it done. Get it done on time.

Accuracy is a variable thing. The new employee must come quickly to realize how much accuracy is required or desired in a situation. Looking back to our anecdote about the student who spent so much time preparing a problem for computer solution, we see that needless accuracy can cost money. On the other hand, if you misplace a decimal point in a seven figure proposal, don't expect much understanding. Acceptance and sympathy with errors decreases as the dollar value of the error increases. Get it done. Get it done on time. Get it done correctly.

Completeness is another factor. Often a question is asked. The answer may be a simple yes or no. But the project of the worker is to supply all necessary or desirable information in support of the answer. Almost any question is open-ended to some extent. But the information cannot be left hanging. It must be as complete as time allows and the importance of the decision requires.

Closure is the "wrapping up" of an assignment. It often involves follow-up, distributing the results of a decision or survey, reporting to the proper supervisors, and can often lead to a whole new project. Lack of closure is the bane of all organizations, and a finely developed sense of closure can be of significant advantage to your future career.

Summary

More jobs are lost because of personal characteristics than by lack of technical ability. The new employee must identify with the employer's goals. He must become rapidly aware of what his employer expects in terms of behavior and ground rules. It is also important to learn the organization both formally and informally. The most immediate attention must be given to the two areas of interpersonal relations and awareness of reality.

Attention must be given to your "image". This involves appearance, manner, and performance. Appearance is a total result of dress, grooming, physical habits, rest, etc. Manner involves loyalty, discretion, tact, poise, and honesty. Performance, among other factors, requires punctuality, accuracy, completeness and closure.

Section II:

Your Future Career Development

We stated much earlier that career development is a continuing process. And so there is no proper end to it. Like time, it goes on and on, running down to a stop of sorts at   retirement, if then.

Like any other process, although the details cannot be seen in advance, the general landmarks are known from the experience of others. As the most important person in your career development, you should give some consideration to the important points.

The first and hardest point to accept is that you, just like all of us, have some limit. There is some point, some challenge, some amount of work, some problem, you will fail at, or fail to accomplish. It is wise, therefore, to set your aspiration level with this in mind. Recognize also that as you move higher in any organization, you begin to see more clearly the strains and pressures as well as the benefits and advantages of higher positions.

Any organization chart is a pyramid. However broad at the base, it is very narrow at the top. *Try*, then, to *balance your aspiration* (the goals you seek) *with your achievements*. But do not merely wait for recognition and progress to come. Instead, constantly assess and evaluate your place and your prospects. Consider, among other things, the following:

Job Equity

We mentioned before that experience builds value, but only to a limited point. By virtue of this, you gain a certain investment value in your job. This is "job equity". For a time, your equity increases fairly rapidly. Then it levels off in many cases. As you approach the leveling off point—i.e., additional experience on the job decreases in value— you might consider either a change of job or a change of employer. In the first case, if you get the next (more responsible) job, you can continue to build equity.

If the next job is not open—or you don't get it, a change of employer may offer one of two things: First, by changing employers you may get the job you want; or second, even if you do not get the particular job you want, you may receive a better salary with a different employer for the same type of job you are now doing.

However, *never change employers without achieving either greater responsibility or more money.* To do the same job twice for the same money has been characterized justly as the harlot's folly. It leads to stagnation and ruin.

Corporation Trends

Beyond your own equity situation, keep a fairly close eye on your employer's development. Any significant change of goals, failure to keep abreast of competition, major shifts of policy, etc., are important to you. The same factor that may offer you opportunity may also be a danger signal. If your boss moves out instead of up, do you really want his job? Look carefully. Maybe you are going to face the same choice later.

In one company we know of, there was an almost unbelievable rate of rise in the copywriting area. Tremendous opportunity. But! After three years, the department head became uncomfortable with everyone. The real secret, of course, was that he wanted to hold his job. Within a ten-year period, no writer ever stayed in the department over four years. The time to get out was during the third year. In the fourth year, the department head found all sorts of reasons for dissatisfaction with anyone. The ability to see this in advance is important. Some companies even have unofficial policies which cull highly paid employees periodically. It is cheaper to feed in at the bottom than to keep experienced personnel beyond the point where their experience is really of value.

In this respect you have advantages by being actively in an organization as an employee, a vantage point you did not have when you took your first job. You are now privy to many new sources of information. Listen. Sympathize. Remember. (Especially remember *Who* said *What*.) Evaluate. Employees of other companies are major sources of information.

Flexibility

In order to implement your own development, you must maintain your flexibility. This means staying abreast of your field, continuing your professional memberships, keeping your lines of communication open. Each new job or assignment must be viewed with this in mind. Some companies, whether accidentally or by design, offer fine financial opportunities at the expense of personal development. Travel, overtime, social affairs, may be great — but find time to keep aware of what you must know to move.

It is useful, as soon as possible, to set a schedule which provides time for reading and activity of a job-connected sort. Again, even at high pay, the alternative is stagnation.

Blockage

Not infrequently career progress can be blocked by accident, interpersonal problems, or external factors. For example of an accidental block: You are hired for a design job which is almost immediately lost to competition. Interpersonal block: Despite basic agreement and respect, you and your boss differ in assessing the direction and rate of change, and he knows it. (Your being correct does not help.) External block: Your family responsibilities suffer from your hours or travel and you feel you must put family first.

When and How to Change Employers or Jobs

Whenever it becomes apparent that your equity is declining or you are faced with stagnation or blockage, you should consider changing either jobs or employers or both.

A job change may be one of progression or direction—never, in the early to middle years, regression. If it is a direction change, i.e. a new job in a new field, you may accept change without salary advantage if necessary. If it is a progression change, it should carry salary increment. Otherwise it will be almost impossible to explain to another prospective employer if you change again.

When change is indicated, discretion and tact are of critical importance. *It is always easier to hunt a job while you have a job.* But be careful that word doesn't get back to your present employer. Sometimes an employer will not only encourage — but assist you in finding a new job. Be sure rather than sorry, though.

Honest and ethical conduct requires that you sell a prospective new employer nothing but yourself. The experience you have gained is yours. Privileged knowledge, however, is not yours to take to a new employer. Failure to accept this restriction can lead to doubt of your integrity, a fatal and permanent flaw in your career development.

Again, there are ground rules in changing jobs. You are responsible for providing adequate notice to your present employer. Unless this is specifically spelled out in your present contract, the minimum acceptable notice is usually the minimum amount of terminal notice your employer provides—generally two weeks to a month.

At higher levels, more notice time is usually specified. It is very uncommon nowadays for any but very small employers (in every sense) to "fire" an employee who gives notice. Transition can be very smooth.

In those fields where annual contracts are provided and barring unusual circumstances, notice should be given at the point of normal contract provision. In other circumstances, opportunity is where it is found.

How much is enough?

A total lack of frustration is an almost nonexistent condition of any job. Again, there are no perfect jobs. On the other hand, when it becomes evident that boredom and lack of change will cause you to stagnate, change is indicated.

Industry is becoming aware of this and employers do not look askance at a person who had two or three employers in five years. If there are six or eight in ten years, however, the attitude changes. You will find that two or three moves should bring you to a satisfying and adequate employer and job situation.

A different kind of job

The majority of college graduates will work for profit-oriented, privately held corporations or businesses of various sizes. A minority will seek either their own business (entrepreneurship) or an individual profession (such as medicine or law). An increasing number will work for non-profit organizations (e.g. private colleges and universities, social agencies, or one of the few non-profit industries) and government agencies of one kind or another—public schools, federal government agencies, police departments, state or local social agencies, etc.

The environments differ to a considerable extent depending on the size, goal and economic structure of the job. In a very real sense, the greater the risk the greater the potential profit. Private professions have the greatest potential income along with owners of businesses. Those who work for private profit-oriented companies come next. Non-profit corporations and governments usually are last in terms of earning potential.

In addition, the degree of structure (definition, formalization) of the environment differs sharply among the categories. The independent professional may do pretty much as he wishes. The employee of private industry may persuade his management that his suggestion will be profitable. The government employee is often bound by cumbersome regulations and, if he is highly innovative, may suffer great frustration.

On the other hand, the government employee need have no thought of his stock-holders. If he is happy at his activity, he need not worry about budget as long as he stays within it. The degree of competition may be more moderate than in personal professions or private industries.

The chart in Appendix A compares general factors of job satisfaction in various career environments.

There are a few somewhat valid rules of change and progress. Note we say "somewhat". No rule applies to all cases; perhaps none applies to yours.

1.   In most areas, the greatest productivity is in the middle forties to late fifties. Because of this . . .

2.   Relatively few changes of employer are successful after the early forties. Therefore . . .

3.   The earlier a specialization is started, or the earlier an administrative sequence is begun, the better for long-term career development.

4.   Any radical change of area or function should take place early in the post-graduate job sequence.

The Sargasso Sea

For all but a very few persons there is an eventual limit to career accomplishment. We cannot each be President or Chairman of the Board. Most of us must, at some point, face the fact that we will not progress much further in our fields; that great public honor will not be ours; that we will neither live nor die in great wealth. We must learn to live with the truth that we have not accomplished and will not accomplish all we dreamed of doing. And, to make matters wholly unacceptable, we finally recognize the fact that we will not live forever.

Many persons, regardless of occupation, sex, values, wealth, et. al., find that this natural limit faces them in the decades of the forties and fifties. In our unique society, age is of value only in moderation. Emphasis is placed in varying degrees on youth, new technologies, new ideas, and only limited value is given to maturity. A technological society tends to place more emphasis on knowledge than on wisdom.

And so it is that many people in middle age face a crisis in self-esteem, in family status, and in career accomplishment, compounded by failing senses, lessening vigor and vitality, moderating and changing enthusiasms and appetites. This period may well be termed a *psychopause,* and it is evidenced by what has been characterized as the middle-aged syndrome. This combination of symptoms and anxieties is most likely to strike in the "fearful forties" or the "fleeting fifties." Unless well understood and adapted to with some understanding and flexibility, it can be fatal to the psyche.

Career progress, if not stalled during this period, is often given undue emphasis as an amelioration of other factors. After all, a man or woman must be useful if he or she is being promoted to vice president even if he or she is confused by his or her children's choices of life style. Unfortunately for many, this period is also characterized by career fixation. In no other society is a person so totally abandoned in middle age as in ours. It is wise, therefore, to foresee and prepare for this time.

Flexibility of personality and variety of interests are the most reliable defenses against disruption and despair during this period. Despite occasionally serious anxiety, the situation of many people is really not as dark as it may seem. Lack of promotion does not always mean lack of personal development. It may be helpful to keep the following in mind when planning:

1. No job should be an end in itself. It is, at best, one of several aspects of accomplishment.

2. The adjustments required in middle life are not a reflection on the individual as much as on the society.

3. It is usually because of past accomplishments that a person faces the limitation of progress. It is easy to move up from the bottom. Only the top is crowded.

4. Status should never be confused with stature. No one on earth can limit what you are—only what you do.

Continuing Education

We have mentioned elsewhere that education continues as long as work. No single element in long term development is more important than a well-planned and faithfully executed program of continuing education. Education helps maintain flexibility. It stimulates the mind, preventing stagnation of initiative.

A well-planned program should include attention to timing and content. Keep in mind a few basics:

1. Prepare educationally for the next job as soon as you have mastered the present one.

2. Prepare in advance for a change of basic job or career direction.

3. Keep fully abreast of technologies related to your field.

4. Keep in mind your "retirement" career.

Retirement

The age of retirement is moving up. It probably will continue to do so. Many people find themselves retired at 55 or 60, relatively comfortable financially but lacking anything useful to do. At this point a second career is often an answer.

In approaching a second career, recognize that you have a great deal more freedom of choice. Your expenses are lower; you have a basic income; you can afford to do what you want. The author does not advocate the second career route for all. If you can afford to fish and like it, fine. But if you want to fish and can't afford to; or can afford to but do not want to, that is our concern.

Because of the large degree of freedom, many persons at this point adopt one of the following solutions:

1. Part-time or full-time social service. This may be paid or unpaid; but, without preparation, even a volunteer is relatively unappreciated.

2. Part-time consulting, especially in an area where a person is a recognized authority.

3. Part-time teaching or research. Some qualification is, of course, necessary.

4. Operation of a small business—e.g., coin-operated carwash or laundromat, motels, gift shops, etc.

The list could go on and on. Let your imagination be your guide. But remember, you are retired now. Leave time to live a little!

APPENDIX A: GENERAL FACTORS OF JOB SATISFACTION IN VARIOUS CAREER ENVIRONMENTS

EMPLOYER

FACTOR	Self-Employed Entre-preneur	Ind. Prof.	Profit Corp. Small	Large	Non-Profit Private	Local	Government State	Federal
Risk (Time - Money)	H	H	H-M	M	H-L	L	L	L
Potential (Money - Status)	H	H	H-L	H-M	M-L	M-L	M-L	M-L
Potential Speed of Realization	H	H	M	M	M	M-L	M-L	M
Frustration Potential (Optimistic)	L-M	L-M	L-H	M	L-H	M	M	M
Degree of Structure	L	L-M	L-M	M-H	M-H	H	H	H
Stability of Income	L	L	M-L	M-H	L-H	H	H	H
Degree of Specialization Likely	M-H	L-H	M-H	H-M	H-M	M-H	M-H	H
Degree of Generalization Feasible	M-H	H	H	H-M	M	M	M	H-M
Degree of Involvement Available	H	H	M-H	L-H	M-H	L-H	L-H	L-H
Necessary Degree of "People" Work	H	H	H-M	M-L	H-M	M-L	M-L	M-L
Necessary Degree of "Thing" Work	M-H	L-H	M	L-M	L-M	L-M	L-M	L-M
Necessary Degree of "Data" Work	M-H	H-M	M-H	M-L	M-L	L	L	L
Range of Activity Level - Physical	H	H	M-H	L-H	L-H	L-H	L-H	L-H
Range of Activity Level - Intellectual	L-H	M-H	M-H	L-H	L-H	M-H	L-H	L-H
Range of Activity Level - Emotional	L-H	M-H	L-H	L-H	M-H	L-H	L-M	L-M

H = High   M = Moderate   L = Low

APPENDIX B: TESTS and TESTING

Fundamentally, a test is a measuring device, similar to a ruler or electric meter. It samples the behavior of a person in the specific test situation. The belief underlying all educational and psychological testing is that the behavior a person exhibits in a test is an indication of his general behavior, and that some of his present behavior can be analyzed to predict his future behavior.

Types of Tests

Tests of Learning - Information Tests

One common test, familiar to every student, is intended to measure the student's retention of previous learning. Such tests are solely information-measuring devices which present some aspects of a previous situation and asks the student to supply other aspects. If he does so correctly, he proves that he has "learned".

Tests of this sort can be found in several forms - from a test of pure recall (the ability to recover previous experience from memory with minimal cueing) to tests of recognition (the ability to recover previous learning when presented with proper and improper alternatives).

Tests of Potential—Ability Tests

A second type of test, with which all college students are familiar, is a test of ability. Such a test attempts to measure the competence or capacity of a person to do something. Tests of physical ability might involve doing a certain number of push ups, chin ups, bends, etc. The ability test in the mental area is often called an aptitude test. In theory, an aptitude test measures a specific mental ability, e.g., scholastic aptitude. It does this by presenting new situations (new learning, in this case) and evaluating the student's behavior in the situation.

Aptitude tests are extensively used in the educational and industrial environment. One whole area of aptitude tests is involved in the admissions programs for graduate schools in medicine, law, education, sciences, etc. In theory, an aptitude test shows not what a person has done, but what he *can* do. In fact, of course, a great deal of what a person can do depends on what he has done.

Intelligence tests are tests of general rather than specific ability. Almost all people admit that there is such a thing as "intelligence", but relatively little agreement can be found in defining it. In general, however, it relates to levels of various "special" abilities, and involves the capacity to remember, to adapt to novel circumstances, to utilize tools of visualization and communication, and to progress in a purposeful way. Creativity - the ability to think and act in new ways, in imaginative ways, is also a factor.

Other factors being equal, verbal and mathematical facility, critical reading skills, logical thinking, and speed of comprehension and perception will lead to high scores on aptitude tests in the areas usually important to the college student or graduate. Experience in taking similar tests can be very valuable, and, used properly, some of the books on the market for preparing for specific tests can be extremely beneficial.

Up to now we have discussed only group tests, i.e., printed tests in which the flexibility of "correct" answers is very limited. Other tests are available, and are used both in the educational and industrial setting, which deal with the individual, and wherein the test administrator exerts some judgment in crediting a specific choice.

These individual tests of ability or intelligence are not simply tests of recollection or choice. To some extent, being individual, they are not objective; rather, they are unique for each person. The same "question" may have several "correct" answers, but the answer the subject chooses tells more about him than that he knows the answer.

Let's look at a type of question: "What does 'Sphere' mean?" One person might say: "Round-solid"- a basic recognition, adequate. A second person might respond: "A surface every point of which is equidistant from a point within called the center" -a textbook definition, adequate. A third might say: "A ball-round-hard"-basic similarity, adequate. Throughout the whole vocabulary section of such a test, a pattern of answers might show up for a person. In addition, to the "correctness" of the answers, the "pattern" can be, and often is, interpreted by the test administrator - and becomes one more aspect of the evaluation. Because of this factor (and others) administration of individual tests is normally restricted to persons who have had substantial supervised experience with the particular devices; persons who have learned how to "interpret" the test. In the hand of unskilled persons, interpretations can be very irregular, and sometimes bizarre conclusions may be derived.

Individual tests of intelligence involve, usually, in addition to "questions" of a verbal nature, some elements of "performance", using things, rather than words. This aspect of the individual test sometimes makes the resulting evaluation more valid, especially for a subject who has language difficulties, or a subject who performs well, but has difficulty expressing answers verbally. It is not uncommon for scores of a single person to vary to some extent between the "verbal" and "performance" sections of a test. Again, only a qualified professional should interpret the meaning of such a variation.

Psychological Tests

While achievement and aptitudes are areas with which the student has had some experience, there are other areas in which tests are used which are likely to be less familiar to him. Tests are constructed to measure, in some ways, the interests, values, attitudes, habits, concerns, and various "psychological" components of personalities of individuals.

The first of these areas—interests—is measurable by comparing interests of persons by groups. Of the available tests in this field, by far the most prevalent in use is the *Strong Vocational Interest-Blank (SVIB)* which is available in forms for men and for women. From samples based on actively employed persons in various careers, common interests can be compared against a number of occupations.

The *SVIB* has been widely enough used at the college level so that a body of interpretive information is available for it. It measures only interest, however, and has no relationship to ability. In this respect, it measures what it claims to.

Interests, since they seem relatively stable after a person reaches the early twenties, are a favorite field of test users. Those companies which still use interest measures in selecting employees assume (sometimes in the face of conflicting evidence) that an interested employee is a more productive employee. The SVIB includes such a wide range of non-job involved interests that it would probably not be a valid measure of specific interest for any of the occupations it lists. This aspect, which renders the test less useful to the company, is no weakness for the student who seeks general areas he may investigate in identifying a broad career orientation. Such tests may be useful to the student in learning more about himself.

Value inventories seek to measure in some construct the aspects of personality and environment a person places the highest premium on. While not extensively used by industry, a value inventory can be useful to the student considering the consistency of his goals and value thinking. For example, persons who persist in choosing medicine as a career are seldom primarily "economic" value oriented, while those leaning toward law or public relations work often are. Tests available in this area are not comparable with each other, each using a different basic model.

Some measures exist of attitudes, which are perceived as more transient and superficial than values. In so far as they may aid the student in considering his real values and attitudes, and their relationship to himself and others, inventories of this sort are useful.

Some tests seek to provide a picture of the "total personality" of an individual. As with the previous inventories of interest and value/attitude, they do this by evaluating the response of the individual to a statement. Most popular (at present) of the personality inventories is the *Minnesota Multiphasic Personality Inventory (MMPI)*. This is a useful instrument in the hands of a capable counselor, but as with other tests, can be dangerous without proper interpretation. The *MMPI* asks the subject to answer T (True); F (False); or ? (Can't say or don't know) to a list of 550 statements. The statements and responses were selected from research done with normal and mentally ill populations, and a profile can be drawn from the instrument on 10 scales. Substantial variation on some scales can be interpreted as indicative of a degree of deviation in certain areas of personality. As with some other devices, there is a built in "honesty" scale, which tends to indicate the person trying to avoid or manipulate the test. The "test" does not measure facts, but rather the response of the subject to a broad range of subjects.

From this point it is only a step to a general technique known as "projective" testing. One type of projective test is the "Draw a Person" test. The figure drawn is interpreted (hopefully by an experienced professional) in terms of its sex, general balance, completeness, clothing, emphases, and omissions, among other things. The artistic quality is not evaluated. The presumption is that the subject, having been told to draw a person, will represent either himself or someone important to him (in general, not specifically) as he thinks about that person.

Varieties of "projective" tests include picture interpretation; diagram completion: "Draw a . . ." (house, man, woman, etc); response to ink blots; "Tell me a story" and other mechanisms. Some interviewers from industry attempt this technique in the interview. The student should be aware of its significance.

While many specific tests exist which are not covered in this section, most will fall in one category or another.

APPENDIX C: SALARY INFORMATION

Salary is not, in most cases, either the most or the least important of the factors of employment. It is, at best, a significant part of income—almost never the only part. For the young graduate especially, it should be viewed in the context of the whole career situation.

Happily, salary—i.e., money income—and attendant benefits represent one aspect of most careers about which a good deal of information can be gained. Unhappily, it is very difficult to make realistic statements this year about next year or the year beyond when discussing salary. Perhaps the best that can be done is to discuss variables and indicate sources of information.

Starting Salary

In general, salary is related to other variables, especially to:

1. **Amount of preparation**: Education / training / experience—e.g., advanced study, especially doctoral study extends average earnings higher and over a longer period.

2. **Risk or security**. As a rule the less secure occupations have a higher potential money income (refer Appendix A). The security of government employment is a factor here, also.

3. **The Nature of the Employer**: Usually the employee who is working in the major field of his employer's emphasis will start higher and progress more rapidly. Widespread corporate diversification is moderating this to some extent.

4. **Selectivity**: Most companies will seek out and pay for the highly qualified graduate. The marginal graduate, as the marginal employee, will likely be offered less.

5. **Demand**: Those disciplines in short supply draw larger salaries, the normal effect of competition.

The only comprehensive and continuing survey of baccalaureate graduates' salaries is done by the College Placement Council. In recent years, inflation has rendered actual figures so transitory as to make them generally useless. Basic differences continue to have some validity, however. The following pages indicate *relative* levels of entry salaries. In 1980 the range from HH to LL was from approximately $1,800 a month to approximately $1,000 a month.

121

APPARENT CURRENT DEMAND/VALUE – BY CURRICULUM

Curriculum	Demand	Dollar Value	Trend
Accounting	H	M	level
Business–general	MH	M	level
Marketing, Distribution	M	M	level
Humanities	L	L	down
Social Sciences – incl. Economics	L	LM	down–level
Engineering –			
Chemical	HH	HH	up!
Civil	M	MH	level
Electrical	H	H	up!
Mechanical	H	H	up
Metallurgical	M	H	level
Petroleum	H	HH	up!
Engineering technology	MH	MH	level–up
Sciences –			
Agricultural	L	L	level–down
Biological	L	L	level–down
Chemical	M	MH	up
Computer	H	H	up!
Health (Medical)	L	L	down
Mathematical	M	MH	up
Physical/Earth	M	MH	up

Key to abbreviations:

    H = High
    M = Moderate
    L = Low

The chart on the previous page offers only generalizations as actual dollar values change rapidly in these inflationary times. Some offers in humanities/social studies may exceed some offers in chemical engineering. On the whole, however, the immediate future market will tend to value the technological specialties and business specialties higher than the generalist areas. This is not a new phenomenon. It has been true for most of this generation.

What is new is the markedly increased competition for certain technical/business graduates, which is creating a much larger gap between high and low in the demand and value scales. This demand gap is evident from one functional area to another, also. Over four-fifths of all offers to graduating seniors are for engineering or business majors (including EDP/computer). The engineering/technology demand should continue. Conversely, the opportunities in public sector services are expected to decline or, at best, remain level in the face of a continuing large number of graduates seeking jobs in that area.

During the past three years — and, predictably, for a few years to come, this emphasis is tending to produce a financial technocracy. Graduates are being hired in some instances at a higher salary than the previous year's graduates are now making. This compression is a serious problem to recruiters and their employing companies.

Part of the dislocation in salary offers may justly be blamed on inflation, but much of it represents a real gap between industrial demand and academic supply. In a sense, the law of supply and demand is driving prices skyward. Graduates should recognize this trend and be prepared for some adjustment when (and if) the supply of graduating specialists equals the demand.

Appendix D: INDEX